PERSUASION

A Practical Guide to Effective Persuasive Speech

W. F. Strong, Ph.D.
Oregon State University

John A. Cook, Ph.D.
Federal Aviation Administration Management Training School

Pamela Maier
Research Assistant

Kendall/Hunt
Publishing Company
Dubuque, Iowa

We dedicate this book to the memory of Professor William Demougeot whose accomplished storytelling and caustic wit made three-hour seminars only minutes long and always memorable. For those who knew him, Dr. De's spirit will be found alive and well in the pages that follow.

Copyright © 1987 by Kendall/Hunt Publishing Company

Library of Congress Catalog Card Number: 87-81556

ISBN 0-8403-4421-X

Printed in the United States of America
10 9 8 7 6 5 4 3 2 1

Contents

Foreword   ix

1 Persuasion: An Introduction   1
Persuasion by Definition   2
    Case 1   2
    Case 2   2
    Case 3   2
    Case 4   3
The Ends of Persuasion   6
    Attitudes   6
    Behavior   6
    Attitude-Behavior Consistency   7
    Reinforcing Attitudes and/or Behaviors   8
    Modifying Attitudes and/or Behaviors   8
    Reversing Attitudes and/or Behaviors   9
Summary   10

2 A Psychology of Persuasion   11
How to Use Cognitive Dissonance Theory   14
Summary   15

3 Source Credibility and Persuasion   17
A Brief Historical Perspective   17
An Analysis of Credibility   18
    Components of Credibility   20
    The Advertising Study   21
    The Debate Study   21
    A Final Thought on Components   22
Three Stages of Credibility   22
    External Credibility   22
    Internal Credibility   23
    Ending Credibility   24
Establishing Credibility as a Persuader   24
Summary   25

4   **Topic Selection and Audience Analysis**   **27**

Topic Selection   27
    Refining the Topic   29
Audience Analysis   30
    Demographics   30
        Age   31
        Sex   32
        Religion   32
        Race   33
    Psychographics   34
        The Likert Scale   35
        The Semantic Differential   35
Summary   37

5   **Research and Development**   **39**

Research   39
    Interviewing   39
    The Popular Media   40
    Retail Book Stores   41
    Corporate and Agency Sources   41
    The Library Investigation   42
        The Card Catalog   42
        The Reader's Guide to Periodical Literature   42
        Government Documents   42
        Computer Searches   42
        Newspapers   43
        References for Quotations and Great Stories   43
        Vital Speeches of the Day   43
        Librarians   44
Persuasive Support   44
    Statistics   45
        Statistical Illustrations   45
        Surveys   48
    Analogies   49
    Examples   50
        Factual Examples   51
        Hypothetical Examples   52
    Testimony   53
Summary   53

6   **Organizing the Persuasive Message**   **55**

Patterns of Arrangement   56
    Chronological Order   56
    Spatial Order   56
    Topical Order   57
    Causal Order   57

     Problem-Solution Order   57
     Pro and Con Order   57
     General to Specific Order   57
     Specific to General Order   58
Techniques for Organizing   58
     Transitions   58
     Internal Summaries and Previews   59
     Interjections   59
     Mnemonic Devices   60
The Motivated Sequence   60
Summary   62

7 Persuasive Introductions and Conclusions   63
Introductions   63
     Occasion-Based Introductions   64
     The Humorous Introduction   65
     The Hypothetical Situation   65
     The Rhetorical Question   66
     The Startling Statement   66
     The Introductory Teaser   67
     Quotations   67
     Stories   67
         The Humorous Story   67
         The Dramatic Story   68
Conclusions   68
Summary   69

8 Visual Support for Persuasive Messages   71
Not All Visuals Are Visual Aids   71
Special Effects Alone Do Not a Speech Make   72
Controlling the Rate at Which Audiences Process Visuals   72
Your Visuals Say More about You Than You Say about Them   73
Remember Murphy's Law   74
Models   74
     Mechanical   74
     Human   75
Slide Projectors   75
Overhead Projectors   76
Drawings   76
Maps   76
Demonstrations   76
Displaying Statistics   77
     The Pie Graph   77
     The Line Graph   77
     The Bar Graph   79
     The Combination Bar Graph and Line Graph   80
Summary   80

9   Making Language Persuasive   81

Identifying   81
    How to Use This Perspective   83
Labeling   84
    How Words Mean   86
    "God" and "Devil" Terms   88
    Euphemisms   89
    Dysphemisms   91
    Polarization   91
    Metaphor   92
Packaging   95
    Antithesis   95
    Repetition   96
    Parallelism   96
    Alliteration   97
    Personification   98
Summary   98

10   Speaking Persuasively   99

How Do I Cope with the Fear of Speaking?   100
    Beginner's Jitters   101
    The Audience Is on Your Side   102
    Reducing Uncertainties   102
    Isometrics   103
    Some Anxiety Is Good   104
Isn't It True That Great Speakers Are Born and Not Made?   105
Persuasion and Quality of Voice   106
What to Do with Hands   107
Achieving a Natural Delivery   108
Using Notes   108
On Memorization   108

11   Argumentation and Debate   111

Advancing and Supporting Claims   112
    Topic Analysis   112
    Argumentative Support   115
    Use of Evidence in Support   117
    Use of Logical Reasoning in Support   118
    Reasoning as Warranted Claim   120
Modifying and Criticizing Claims   123
    The Process of Refutation   124
    Attacking the Proof   125
    Specialized Fallacies   127
Summary   128

12 **Free Speech and Persuasion** by Ron Manuto **129**
The Values of Free Speech   131
The Espionage Act, 1917   132
President Wilson and Dissent   133
Passage and Enforcement   134
The Supreme Court   137
Limits of Free Speech   138
Basic Legal Doctrines of Free Speech   139
Conclusion   141

Appendix A   143
Appendix B   145

Index   147

Foreword

Although this section of a book is traditionally called the "foreword," its funtion is to foreshadow or forewarn, to prepare the reader for what is to come, to put the book into perspective, to boast, to apologize, to enhance, to explain, to blame, to color, to sell. We will do a little of all of these things.

This book goes against the tide of current textbooks in persuasion. Whereas most persuasion texts published in the last decade have been written for advanced, theory-based courses, this text is unabashedly a handbook for an introductory, performance-based course in persuasive speaking. Focusing largely on the practical needs of the persuasive speaker has allowed us to give the subject a more complete treatment than the one or two chapters that most public speaking texts can afford. Thus, we can stress such things as:

- Making Language Persuasive
- Designing Visuals that Persuade
- Packaging Statistics Persuasively
- Speaking Persuasively
- Persuasive Ordering of Arguments

In saying that we have written a "handbook," we do not wish to imply that this text is devoid of theory. True, we have maximized practice and minimized theory, as a performance-oriented text must do, yet we have included theory when we felt that we could help students put it to practical use. For instance, we have always felt that cognitive dissonance theory is most useful in analyzing speeches, but we never felt that there was sufficient explanation, in most texts, on how to put it to use. So in Chapter Two we have painstakingly explained to students how cognitive dissonance theory, when practically applied, can add power to their arguments. We have tried to do the same with every theory we have covered.

This book has a student bias. For this it is both strong and weak. We have endeavored to identify, identify, identify with what a student faces in selecting a speech topic, researching it, organizing it, and delivering it. Furthermore, we have labored under a philosophy which says that when we wish to illustrate a theory or a principle of persuasion we will use, whenever possible, examples that are no more than four years old. Thus, we have included excerpts from the speeches of contemporary speakers like Jesse Jackson, Mario Cuomo, Ronald Reagan, and Garry Trudeau. Yet we have not sold out completely to the modern world. There are times when the persuasive styles of Webster or Churchill or Malcolm X cannot be surpassed, so we have relied upon the time-honored, master orators as well. We have drawn on modern advertising and advertisements not only to identify with students, but also to demonstrate to them that the principles discussed herein are not just academic relics with which we insist on torturing them, but principles in use all around them because they are effective. All of this we have tried to do with good humor. To whatever extent we have failed in this regard, it is my co-author's fault.

The strength of this book, we hope, is that students will find that it speaks directly to them and their problems. Thus, we hope to release new editions of this book every two years in order to maintain a strong level of idenitfication with the students who use it.

No book, no matter how heavily footnoted, adequately credits all those who are responsible for its existence. We will thank those whom we know had an influence and apologize in advance to those whom we manage to slight.

We thank our professors at North Texas State University who taught us and inspired us nearly a decade ago, Ted Colson, William DeMougeot, to whom this book is dedicated, Tom Hurt, Will Powers, and Victoria O'Donnell. We especially thank Victoria O'Donnell because she nurtured our interests in the art and science of persuasion.

We thank Lloyd Crisp, Chairman of the Department of Speech Communication at Oregon State University for his sharp editorial eye and for his even sharper running-commentary in the margins of rough drafts. Ron Manuto, too, we thank whole-heartedly for his guest-authoring of the final chapter on "Freedom of Speech," which is his area of expertise, not ours.

We thank Pamela Maier for her tireless research and permissions efforts. We thank Craig Galloway, Ron Boggs, Darvin Malone, and Patti Peshka, all of whom loaned us their beautiful faces for the photographs in the "Delivery" chapter. We, of course, thank E. Alex Mitchell for taking the beautiful photographs of those beautiful faces. Christi Croghan, too, helped a great deal in the final preparation of the manuscript. We thank her.

Most of all we thank our 3000 students, from whom we have collectively heard nearly 10,000 speeches, some brilliantly inspiring, some tolerable, and some horrendous. For those of you who were the latter, but became the former, we genuinely thank you, wherever you are, for you have been our finest teachers.

Strong & Cook, 1987

*Our Creator Himself has Taught us the
Value of Silence by Putting us
Speechless into the World—
If we Learn to Talk Later, we do it
at Our Own Risk.*
                    —Mark Twain

Persuasion: An Introduction

1

Persuasive speech will touch your life many times today. There is very little around you that is not, at least to some extent, the result of persuasive speech. This book is a case in point. During an informal meeting with our editor, we convinced her that there was a market for such a text and that our treatment of the subject would appeal to that market. Your university is the result of persuasive speech, formal and informal, that convinced tax-payers and legislators and donors and foundations that the institution should be built. If you own a car it is likely the result of persuasive speech. No doubt you delivered one of the most persuasive speeches of your life the day you convinced your parents to let you have one.

In the future, you will have many more chances to use persuasive speech. The success or failure of your efforts will affect dramatically the kind of life you will live. Some of your efforts will be relatively unimportant, such as trying to convince your algebra professor to give you a "B" instead of a "C" for basic algebra. Some efforts will be highly significant, such as trying to persuade an interviewing panel that you should be admitted to law school or medical school. Some efforts will seem vital, like convincing a fine company that you are the right person that $40,000-a-year marketing position. Before you know it, you will go full-circle and find yourself on the other side of the car issue, needing to persuade your own teen-agers that car ownership is something that they they are too young and inexperienced to assume.

Since persuasive speech, like communication, is all about us, why should we need to study it? After all, we have been consumers and producers of persuasive speech since early childhood. Surely in a society such as ours one is skilled in persuasion by the age of 18! Though this seems to make sense, it is just not the case. At this moment, someone well over 18 is being swindled out of thousands of dollars because of a manipulative and unscrupulous sales representative. The person being swindled does not know how to recognize invalid arguments and does not know the questions to ask that might reveal them. Thus, the study of persuasive speech performs an important "defensive" purpose. It helps us defend ourselves against irrational and spurious claims. Conversely, as teachers of persuasive speech, we have all too often recognized how poorly and ineffectively students present even the simplest "offensive" argument. Virtually every term we have students request a make-up exam using this argument: "I couldn't study for your test because I had to study for Chemistry." Do the students believe that admitting a preference for chemistry should earn them the preferential treatment of a make-up exam for a course they slighted? The argument sabotages itself. Naturally, such poor uses of persuasive speech extend beyond the university gates.

Spend a day in any traffic court and you will hear new varieties on this weak theme. Defendants will argue that they should not have to pay their parking tickets because "parking tickets aren't fair." Or they will claim that they were only speeding because they were "running out of gas."

It is the pervasiveness of such ineffective and naive persuasive speech strategies that creates the need for formal study in this area. When you have completed this book and the course that it accompanies, it is our hope that you will have an improved ability to design and deliver effective and ethical persuasive messages. It is also our hope that through the study of "offensive" methods of persuasive speech, you will learn important lessons about how to protect yourself from, and even counter, misleading and false persuasive claims.

PERSUASION BY DEFINITION

Perhaps the best way to understand what peruasion is and what it is not is to look at several cases in which compliance was gained by a variety of means.

Case 1

17 U.S. F-111 bombers streak over Tripoli on a midnight raid, dropping tons of bombs on alleged terrorist training and supply centers. Dozens of people are killed, including Libyan leader, Muammar el-Qaddafi's baby daughter. In succeeding months there is an apparent lull in terrorist activities in Europe. Supposing that Qaddafi was the primary supporter of terrorism in Europe, has the bombing persuaded him to give up his terrorist ways?

Case 2

The federal government of the United States believes that the legal drinking age should be 21 on a national basis. Since each state has the right to establish its own legal drinking age, the federal government mandates that any state that does not enact and enforce a legal drinking age of 21 will lose millions of dollars in federal highway funds. Most states comply with the mandate. Would you say that the federal government has persuaded the states to change the legal drinking age to 21?

Case 3

A lawyer places a rape victim on the witness stand and, having no means of defending his client, who is charged with the rape, proceeds to ask these questions which he knows are unfounded:

"Isn't it true that you were known to be an exhibitionist when you were a cheerleader in high school?"

"Isn't it true that, during college, you regularly "entertained," and I use the word in its broadest sense, potential scholarship athletes who visited the campus?"

"And isn't it also true that you approached the defendant on more than one occasion, asking him to come to your apartment when his wife was out of town?"

"One more question. Did you or did you not once tell your office co-workers that you divorced your first two husbands because they were not 'exciting' enough —in your words, 'had no sense of fantasy.?' "

2

The woman runs from the stand in tears. Later that day she drops the charges against the defendant because she cannot endure the humiliation of the defense attorney's questions. Has the defense attorney persuaded the court of his client's innocence?

Case 4

You get off the plane and begin walking down the airport concourse when a handsome young man in an orange robe approaches you and pins a flower on your lapel. He says, "Could you give me a quarter to help build our church?" You say "No." The young man walks beside you down the concourse. He is smiling. He asks again, "Will you not give a quarter to help do the Lord's work?" You say, "No." He stays with you all the way down to the baggage department, constantly asking for the quarter. Finally, you stop and dig into your pocket and give him a quarter. He blesses you and leaves. Have you been persuaded to give him a quarter?

In each case, the desired goal was reached; terrorism was curbed, laws amended, a client's freedom gained, and a quarter earned. Yet do the ends achieved require that we regard each case as an illustration of persuasion? Of course not. At the heart of persuasion, as it has been traditionally defined, is "free will." For persuasion to be persuasion, the person or audience being persuaded must be free to accept or reject the argument presented. The person or audience must be free to comply with or refuse to comply with the action requested. It is a truism that "a man persuaded against his will is of the same opinion still." Thus, U.S. bombers may *force* Qaddafi to quit supporting terrorism, but they may not *persuade* him to think of it as an undesirable means of fighting the imperialists. The federal government might econmically coerce states into raising the legal drinking age, even though legislators in those states may continue to believe that 18 or 19 is a reasonable age at which one should be able legally to drink. In the third case, the lawyer used emotional coercion to force the rape victim to retract her charges. Most astute jurors would recognize the ploy for what it was and remain unconvinced of the defendant's innocence. Finally, the religious zealot who manipulated a quarter out of you at the airport did so by means of interpersonal coercion. He annoyed you to the point of compliance.

None of the four cases we have examined could be called an example of "pure" persuasion. A helpful means of knowing whether something is or is not a case of "pure" persuasion is to look at why compliance was gained. In case one Qaddafi ceased his terrorist ways for fear of losing his life. Case two gains compliance from the states because good roads are precious, political commodities for legislators. Neither of the first two cases are examples of "pure" persuasion. Case one is "pure" coercion and case two is close. The third case is not as easy to call. The lawyer does not physically torture the defendant to get her to withdraw the charges, yet neither is his strategy designed for a free and open inquiry of his client's innocence. We must regard the third case as an example of what we might call coercive-persuasion. Finally, we must conclude that the religious zealot is practicing coercive-persuasion as well. Most people do not give him quarters because they want to help him "build his church." Most do it to buy freedom from his persistence and obnoxiousness.

For a clearer idea of the differences between coercion and persuasion, both means of gaining compliance, study the chart below.

COMPLIANCE GAINING STRATEGIES

Coercion	Persuasion
Forced Compliance (includes)	Free Compliance (includes)
Physical Harm	Reasoning
Jail	Arguments
Black Mail	Appeals
Terrorism	Pleading
Economic Sanctions	Bargaining
Threats	Promises
War	

Though divisions such as these help us understand conceptually the differences between coercion and persuasion, in practice, the two must overlap at times. As Wheeless, et al., have observed, ". . . coercion uses elements of persuasion, just as persuasion may utilize elements of coercion" (1983). In short, few people are motivated to change belief or behavior on the basis of reason alone. Changes occur due to implied and specified rewards and punishments that will be the result of compliance or non-compliance.

As a teen-ager, your mother may have encouraged you to clean your room by saying, "You don't want to live in a pig sty do you?" If you were like most teen-agers, you were quite pleased with your personal pig sty. However, you probably cleaned your room anyway because you realized that your mother had the power to provide rewards and punishments that could make your life either perfect or perfectly miserable. Thus, she persuaded you to comply with her wishes due to her coercive potential.

Even in cases of greater freedom to accept or reject a persuasive appeal, some coercive elements are present. Susan read an advertisement for a sensational, high-fiber diet that promised good health and quick and painless weight-loss. She tried the diet not because of the health benefits, but because she believed that losing weight would make her more attractive to men. Simultaneously she was responding to reward (a thin figure would make her more desirable) and avoiding punishment (being over-weight would hurt her socially). Though we might conclude that Susan is being socially coerced into this kind of thinking, her decision to go on the diet is about as free-willed as one can get. She is quite free to accept or reject the diet.

To this point we have examined the three major parts of the compliance-gaining continuum. These include coercion, coercive-persuasion, and persuasion (see figure 1.1). Coercion, in its purest sense, is that which includes forced compliance through physical domination. Coercive-persuasion ranges from threats of violence ("Do what I say and you won't get hurt") to unspoken potential for punishing and rewarding ("We better keep the boss happy by doing it her way"). Persuasion, in its purest sense, is gaining the compliance of a one who is completely free to comply or not to comply with the persuasive message.

COERCION	COERCIVE-PERSUASION	PERSUASION

Figure 1.1

4

This book is concerned primarily with the right side of this continuum. Since we have come to an understanding of persuasion by focusing on what it is not, we should now turn to a consideration of what it is. As is true of any discipline, definitions of persuasion are plentiful. Not surprisingly, such definitions range from the simplistic to the incredibly complex. There is no need to examine all the intricacies of such definitions when we are concerned primarily with the most practical elements of persuasive speech. Consequently, the following list of practical definitions is provided as a foundation for the perspectives to be discussed in this book.

1. Persuasion is the process of inducing auditors, through the use of facts, logic, rationalization, or emotional appeal, to change their minds and attitudes, deepen existing feelings, or proceed to actions in which they would otherwise not engage (Oliver, 1950, p. 8).
2. Persuasion is "the cocreation of a state of identification or alignment between a source and a receiver that results from the use of symbols" (Larson, 1986, p. 8).
3. Persuasion is a complex, continuing, interactive process in which a sender and a receiver are linked by symbols, verbal and nonverbal, through which the persuader attempts to influence the persuadee to adopt a change in a given attitude or behavior because the persuadee has had his perceptions enlarged or changed (O'Donnell & Kable, 1982, p. 9).

Oliver's definition is linear in nature. It is too easy to conclude from such a definition that persuasion is a source-centered activity wherein a persuader creates a powerful message and virtually injects it into an audience that will respond appropriately if there is a proper mix of facts and logic and emotional appeal. Oliver himself would be the first to say that it just is not that easy. If it were, we would simply publish a long list of formulas to which speakers could go to get the right strategy for the right situation. We must read Oliver's definition through the filter of the other two to give it its needed scope. Larson, and O'Donnell and Kable, both provide the "interactive" dimension of persuasion, thus giving the audience a larger role in the process. In other words, I cannot persuade you by myself. I need your help. You can either pay attention or not pay attention, accept or reject my appeals according to your sense of logic or lack of logic, and take or not take the action that I request because of a whole myriad of beliefs and prejudices within you that I can never know. What you are determines more about the meaning of my message than anything I put into it. This is why there is such a dire need for insightful, audience analysis on the part of the persuader. The more we know about our audiences, the better we can predict how they will respond to our messages.

It is traditional to make a distinction between concious and non- concious cases of gaining compliance. If Kristen begins wearing her hair like Cindi Lauper, or begins wearing clothes of 16 different colors, none of which match, can we conclude that Cindi has persuaded her to change her hair style or to take fashion risks? No, Kristen is modeling Cindi's behavior, but Cindi did not conciously seek Kristen's compliance.

There are many such incidents of modeling behavior on the part of fans. Sometimes it is completely unexpected, as when Clark Gable wore no undershirt in a popular movie of the 1930's and sent undershirt sales plummeting; at other times it is conciously planned, such as the time that Burt Reynolds sold so many Trans Ams by means of his wild driving antics in "Smokey and the Bandit." Similarly, "E. T." purposefully boosted sales of Reeses' Pieces. When such results are unplanned and unconcioulsy achieved, we cannot conclude that persuasion has occurred. However, when modeling behavior is encouraged by means of a concious strategy, then persuasion has been achieved. Why the need for this distinction? If we do not know what persuasive ends we have in mind and by what means we plan to achieve them, how can we know whether or not our persuasive strategy has been effective? Cases of gaining compliance accidentally are fortunate, but until we can explain what caused that "accident" and predict what will happen in similar circumstances in the future, we cannot systematically use the "accident" to our advantage.

THE ENDS OF PERSUASION

Persuasion allows us several options. We can seek to *reinforce* existing attitudes and/or behaviors; to *modify* existing attitudes and/or behaviors, or to *reverse* existing attitudes and/or behaviors. Prior to discussing each option in detail, we should have a working definition of attitude, behavior, and how the two interact.

Attitudes

An attitude is a "relatively enduring predisposition to respond favorably or unfavorably to an idea, object, or behavior" (O'Donnell & Kable, p. 35). For instance, when we say that Craig has a bad attitude, we mean that, in general, Craig is predisposed to being negative about everything. Before we even suggest that he come with us to see the film, "Platoon," we know that he is going to react negatively to the idea. He will find some excuse not to go. He will say, "All those Vietnam movies are boring."

Most of us, however, are not always negative. Neither are we positive about everything. Our attitudes are different according to different issues and situations. We ask our friends for their opionions, which are attitudes made public. We will ask, "How do you stand on the Nicaragua question?" "Do you think that high schools should distribute birth control?" "Is a compact disc really better than a cassette tape?" We want to know how they are predisposed to responding to many things. In this way we shape and alter our own attitudes, as well as shaping and altering theirs.

Tremendous amounts of money and energy are spent every day in this country simply to ascertain and monitor public attitudes. Political pollsters want to know how the majority of Americans feel about the idea of a decrease in the defense budget and an increase in social programs funding. Such information can be used on the floor of congress to influence legislative voting patterns. Marketing managers talk about attitudes in terms of "image." The collective attitudes of a target market concerning a given automobile amount to an image for that car. Advertising is then designed to maintain or alter that image. Even in the college classroom, students' attitudes about the courses they take and the professors that teach them are ascertained through end-of-term evaluations. Such data are of tremendous value to those professors who take them seriously.

Behavior

Behavior, unlike attitude, is easy to define. A behavior is an action. Naturally, just as a great deal of money is spent on attitude assessment and adjustment, even greater amounts of money are spent to influence behavior. Knowing that 57 percent of Americans are against funding the Contra-rebels in Nicaragua is of little value if politicians cannot get those same Americans to *act* on the basis of that attitude, to vote for candidates who are against funding or to pressure incumbents to vote against such aid. Likewise, convincing a target market that a Volvo is an unusually safe car is of no value to Volvo if they cannot get consumers to act on that image and *buy* the car. Consequently, professional persuaders invest most of their time and money attempting to induce action. The Red Cross wants you to donate blood, the Department of Transportation wants you to wear your seat-belt, the Sierra Club wants you to take care of our natural resources, Budweiser asks that you buy their beer, and David Letterman pleads with you to stay up late and watch his show. The minute-by-minute barrage is endless. Even the sales organizations themselves spend vast sums of money to acquire the world's best motivational speakers to inspire their sales representatives to make more calls and work longer hours to achieve success for themselves and their companies.

Attitude-Behavior Consistency

Is there a relationship between attitude and behavior? If Brent is against legalizing the sale of alcohol on campus and the majority of students vote it in, will Brent subsequently refuse a beer when the on-campus pub is open for business? Clearly, it depends on a many factors. How strong was his opposition in the first place? Did he oppose it because of deeply-held religious convictions that drinking is wrong? Does his belief in the sanctity of majority rule negate his original objections? Is the beer free?

The question of attitude-behavior consistency has troubled social- scientists for years. Originally, it was believed that if people reported on an attitude survey that they were strongly in favor of a highway litter clean-up bill, that they would not behave in ways that would add to the highway litter problem. Studies have shown, however, that such an assumption is often wrong. The very people who support an anti-litter bill may be seen throwing apple cores out their car windows because they believe that apple cores are not trash. "Birds eat them," they might say. Clearly, this action is inconsistent with our conception of an anti-litter attitude, but not inconsistent with theirs, because, for them, apple cores are not trash. This example points to the complexity of conducting accurate and useful attitudinal research. Still, there are more blatant cases of attitude-behavior inconsistency. Many smokers have a negative attitude about their smoking habit and yet continue to smoke. Those who regularly use tanning beds may believe that such beds are dangerous, and yet they continue to pursue the perfect, golden glow. Does this mean that attitudes, as a concept, are of no value to the would-be persuader? No. It means simply that attaining consistency between attitudes and behaviors may depend upon our ability to identify all the attitudes that cause or support a given behavior. As Herbert Simons illustrates, ". . . any given behavioral act seems to be the product of not one but several attitudes. Whether we sign a petition to save the California redwoods, for example, may be determined not only by our attitude toward the redwoods, but also by our attitude toward the act of signing petitions and toward the person who solicits our signature" (1986, p. 64). Thus, the low correlation between attitude and behavior teaches us that we may find it easy to convince someone that they should run a mile every day. Getting that person to actually put on the running shoes and endure the inevitable agony of the first week of running is quite another matter.

Reinforcing Attitudes and/or Behaviors

Were we to ask most people to define persuasion they would say that it deals with *changing* the attitudes and behaviors of others. The problem with this popular notion is that it ignores the most common function of persuasion, which is *reinforcing* existing attitudes and behaviors. Most advertising, for instance, is designed not to get people who drink Budweiser to drink Miller Lite, but rather, to keep those who now drink Miller Lite drinking Miller Lite. In other words, the aim of most advertising is simply to maintain market share, to reinforce desired consumer behavior.

Many of the institutions to which we belong serve to reinforce our attitudes and behaviors. You will not hear much about a college degree being worthless while attending a university. It is in the self interest of the university to keep students who believe in the value of education right on believing in it. Churches, too, are healthiest when they are able to inspire parishoners to regular attendance. "Don't forsake the assembly" ministers and priests often say. Through regular attendance, members are spiritually reinforced. When their attendance falls off, they are vulnerable to competing persuasions.

Our friends function as a kind of informal institution that reinforces our attitudes and behaviors. This is why our parents are naturally concerned about our being "influenced" by "the wrong crowd." They know how incredibly strong peer pressure can be. Consequently, for some people to change an undesired behavior, such as kicking an addiction to cocaine, they have to escape the influence of the friends that reinforce that behavior.

It is good to think about all the subtle ways in which our attitudes and behaviors are reinforced. The most enduring, controlling forces in our lives are those that we do not perceive as such. Denial of influence and control is a clue that complete surrender has occurred. Give it some thought. In what ways are your attitudes and behaviors reinforced by advertising, institutions, and friends? What influences do you deny, and are you being honest with yourself?

Modifying Attitudes and/or Behaviors

Another popular notion about persuasion is that it concerns changing people from a position of being for something to being against it, or vice-versa. This notion is unrealistic, particularly if we consider that a person or audience may be strongly opposed to our position and we have only five minutes to convert them. However, if we can get a person or audience to at least "see our point" we have made some headway. This "headway" we define as one kind of persuasion.

Suppose you are a representative of the athletic department at a major university. Your department depends on the student council for 25 percent of its funding through student fees. This year, you have heard that most of the students on the council believe that the money spent on athletics is excessive and wasteful. Some propose cutting your budget by as much as 50 percent. You are assigned by the Director of the Athletic Department to save the funding. What do you do? You first conduct a survey of the attitudes of those on the council. You need to know, after all, just where you stand. After compiling the data you learn that things are not as bad as they seemed. True, four members of the council are polarized on the issue, dead set against athletics. Collectively, however, the council has a mean of only 3.9. When the polarized respondents are thrown out, you see that the adjusted mean is 3.4 (see figure 1.2). Consequently, in your address, you focus on those who represent the adjusted mean. After your eloquent speech, you conduct another survey and discover that you shifted the targeted audience's attitudes to a new mean of 3.2. When the vote is taken later that week, the athletic department budget is reduced by only 3

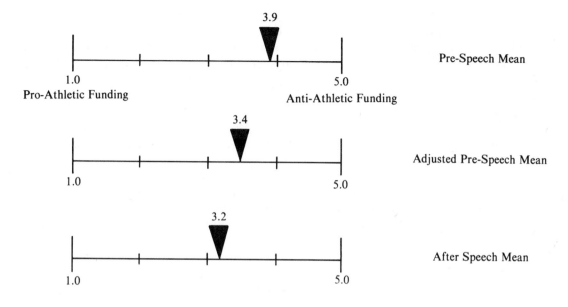

Figure 1.2

percent. Did you fail? Probably not. It is more likely that your brilliant strategy saved the athletic department from a much larger budget cut. Your speech must be regarded, then, as a successful persuasive effort, even though you only altered attitudes rather than converting them completely to your side.

Behavior, like attitudes, sometimes needs to be modified. There are numerous times when we seek only to alter another's behavior, not to extinguish it altogether. For instance, a woman may want her husband to watch less baseball on weekends, a young man may request that his girlfriend spend fewer nights "out with the girls," or a medical expert may encourage a television audience to significantly reduce its consumption of dairy products. In each case, the persuader does not ask for the persuadee(s) to give up the given behavior completely. The persuader asks only for a reduction.

Reversing Attitudes and/or Behaviors

Here we wish to make a distinction between modifying and reversing. To modify is to alter while to reverse means to change completely or to extinguish. Sometimes modification will not do. Many companies are discovering that merely setting up smoking areas is not an adequate means of coping with the second-hand smoke controversy. Some corporations are going so far as to decree that those employees who do not quit smoking must quit their jobs. Such decrees do not ask for modification of behavior, they demand behavioral extinction.

When Martin Luther King directed the great bus boycott in Montgomery, Alabama, in 1955, he did not persuade the blacks of that city to ride the bus only once a day or once a week; he persuaded them not to ride the bus at all. He asked for, and received, a complete reversal of behavior on the part of the black citizens of Montgomery. It was an astonishing victory for King.

After all, it was by bus that most blacks traveled back and forth to work. For over a year, the black community stuck together and walked and car-pooled and bicycled to work until the policy that sanctioned segregation on the buses was revoked. It was essential to King's larger goals that he convince the black community not simply to alter, but to thoroughly reverse its bus-riding behavior.

SUMMARY

In this chapter we have demonstrated that persuasive speech is a vital part of our lives, no matter what life we live. The study of persuasion has both an "offensive" and "defensive" purpose. Persuasion is to be distinguished from coercion, though there are situations wherein the two overlap a good deal. This book is concerned with the ethical dimensions of persuasion and coercive-persuasion. There are at least three general goals of persuasion: to reinforce existing attitudes and/or behavior, to modify existing attitudes and/or behavior, and to reverse or extinguish existing attitudes and/or behavior.

REFERENCES

Larson, C. U. (1986). *Persuasion: reception and responsibility.* Belmont, California: Wadsworth Publishing Company.

O'Donnell, V., & Kable, J. (1982). *Persuasion: an interactive-dependency approach.* New York: Random House.

Oliver, T. T. (1968). *The psychology of persuasive speech.* New York: David McKay Company, Inc.

Simons, H. W. (1986). *Persuasion: understanding, practice, and analysis.* New York: Random House.

Wheeless, L. R., Barraclough, R., & Stewart, R. (1983). Compliance gaining and power in persuasion. *Communication Yearbook 7* 105–145.

A Psychology
of Persuasion

2

There are a tremendous number of common expressions for states of craziness. Here are a few:

His elevator doesn't go all the way to the top.

He's not playing with a full deck.

She doesn't have all her oars in the water.

The lights are on but nobody's home.

He's about half a bubble off (a carpenter's expression).

She's a brick shy of a load.

They don't have all their dogs barking.

She's off her rocker.

He's slipped his gears.

He doesn't have all his thrusters firing (from Star Trek Iv).

We use such expressions to creatively describe the condition of one who is "a little off." In fact, if we study these examples carefully, we see that they all allude to a condition where things are not quite right, where things are a bit out of balance, out of sync, needing repair. The prevalence and widespread use of these phrases teaches us something especially important about ourselves. We like for things to be balanced, fit, and in full working order. If they are not, we feel pressure to to set them right.

You can verify this assertion from your own experience. Have you ever been in a room where a badly tilted picture was hanging on the wall? Didn't you want to straighten it? How about talking to someone whose glasses were crooked? Did you find it difficult to pay attention to what that person was saying? In both cases you were disturbed by visual inconsistency, and you wanted, even needed, to put things back in balance.

We react to the world of ideas the same way we react to the physical world around us. We like for ideas to be balanced and consistent, too. This is the reason that most people who seek to convince others of their wrong-headedness will attempt to point out inconsistencies in their beliefs, values, and behavior. "Look," they will say, "you can't be against nuclear power and for nuclear missiles! That's inconsistent!" Or they might say, to their congressman, "How can you live with yourself after you cut social security by 2% and gave yourself a 12% raise!" The same strategy is even used by teenagers on their parents: "Why can't I stay out til 1:00? When David was my age he got to stay out til 1:00!" Such arguments ask the inconsistent thinker to "get all his ducks in a row."

This perspective leads us quite naturally to a consideration of one of the most useful theories of persuasion, the theory of cognitive dissonance. Leon Festinger developed his cognitive dissonance theory in the early 1950's. Since then, it has proved useful to all nature of persuasive efforts, from door-to-door sales to political campaigns, from selling cars to selling equal rights.

If you can first understand "dissonance," you will grasp the general theory without much difficulty. Perhaps you first became aquainted with dissonance in terms of sound and feel. A scene in the original *Jaws* movie centered around a semi-hysterical crowd that had gathered in a small room. They were attempting to discuss ways of getting rid of the shark. With everyone talking and screaming at once, nothing was getting accomplished. A salty old fisherman, played by Robert Shaw, strolled over to the chalk board and scraped his inordinately long fingernails down the length of the board. The dissonant sound silenced the crowd. Similarly, many a young musician has driven his family from the house with dissonant notes, notes that were far from harmonic. Other things cause dissonance by feel. Biting down on aluminum foil or a fudge bar stick are sources of dissonance.

Cognitive dissonance is similar to sensory dissonance. The only difference is that cognitive dissonance is mental. It can result from logical inconsistency or from behavior that is in contradiction with your self-concept (Festinger, 1957, p. 14). If you believe that you are a law-abiding citizen and yet drive 75 mph on long trips, you have a contradiction in attitude and behavior. This is a dissonant situation that may not cause dissonance because you can rationalize that "everybody else does it." However, were you to decide to drive 90 mph, you would likely have a tough time rationalizing away the dissonance since the mental distance between "law-abiding" and "90 mph" is too great to justify (see figure 2.1).

Many smokers are finding it difficult to continue smoking in the face of overwhelming evidence of its dangers. Those who are unable to give up a two-pack-a-day habit may reduce the inconsistency of wanting to live a long, healthy life and smoking, by switching to low-tar cigarettes. In this way, the inconsitency is reduced to a point that rationalization becomes effective. The smoker can say, "These aren't dangerous, they're not *real* cigarettes."

Thus, cognitive dissonance may be reduced in one of four ways:

1. Alter the behavior so that it conforms to the attitude.
2. Alter the attitude so that it conforms to the behavior.
3. Alter both the attitude and the behavior to a more comfortable, middle position.
4. Use rationalization, a process wherein one seeks positive information that supports the action taken and avoids negative information that might fault it. (Festinger, pp. 18–24)

Since cognitive dissonance is most clearly observed after we make important decisions, it would be helpful to examine it in light of a decision that has caused tremendous dissonance for many college students: getting engaged.

From the moment that you make the committment to get engaged you will begin to experience some dissonance because of the attractiveness of the alternative decision, staying single. Getting engaged changes your self-image as a single, independent person. Strangely enough, causing engaged couples as much dissonance as possible about their decision to leave the marvelous, single's life is a tradition in this culture. "You'll never get to go out with the guys again" and "It'll be dishes and dirty diapers from now on" are comments intended to cause as much anxiety as possible. You can cope with this post-decisional dissonance by rationalizing that your friends are "just kidding" (which they aren't), or, more effectively, you can seek out those friends that are truly supportive of marriage (engaged or married themselves) and avoid those who will make fun of your decision.

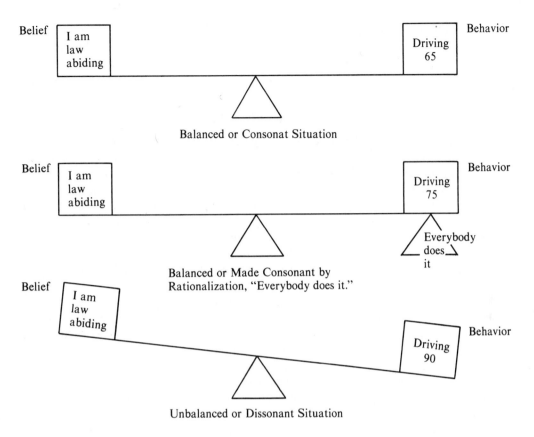

Belief — I am law abiding — Driving 65 — Behavior

Balanced or Consonat Situation

Belief — I am law abiding — Driving 75 — Behavior

Everybody does it

Balanced or Made Consonant by Rationalization, "Everybody does it."

Belief — I am law abiding — Driving 90 — Behavior

Unbalanced or Dissonant Situation

Figure 2.1

The theory of cognitive dissonance has proven very beneficial for automobile marketing. As you know, deciding to buy a car is a major decision for most of us. So let's go through a hypothetical case of you buying a new car to see how the dissonance might affect you. Let's suppose that you have test driven all the great driving machines in the $20,000 to $24,000 range. You have narrowed the field down to the Mazda RX–7 and the BMW–325is. You figure that all things are about equal and just go with a "gut feeling" and buy the BMW. Dissonance will now set in because you have made a choice between two appealing options. How will you reduce this post-decisional dissonance? You will do it by selectively exposing yourself to information that will endorse your decision. Where will you get such information? Besides the arguments given to you by the salesperson, which will circulate in your head for some time, and besides the information in the owner's manual, you will likely find reinforcement for your choice in magazine advertisements. Advertisers know that consumers suffer from post-decisional dissonance and therefore create ads to help consumers feel good about their choices after the fact. This is a particularly vital function of marketing staffs since most customers buy on emotion, but own on logic. In other words, many of us buy first and find out why we bought later. Just talk to someone the day that he or she buys a car, and a month later. A month later that person will have all kinds of new and intelligent "reasons" for making that choice, reasons "learned" after the fact, not before. Hence, the art of marketing is at least partially the art of pre-packaging dissonance reduction information. The information can be communicated in the actual sales presentation so that the customer can call it up later and "rationalize" the choice, or it can be put into the form of advertisements and placed in magazines or newspapers that the customer reads.

HOW TO USE COGNITIVE DISSONANCE THEORY

Upon first learning about cognitive dissonance theory, students often reply, "Well, it's interesting, but what do I do with it? How can I use it in a persuasive speech?" The remainder of this chapter will be devoted to addressing this concern.

Leon Festinger himself has claimed that "cognitive dissonance is a motivating state of affairs. Just as hunger impels a person to eat," he wrote, "so does dissonance impel a person to change his opinions or his behavior" (1977, p. 111). This means that no persuasion can take place until some degree of dissonance is experienced by the audience. Without dissonance, the audience has no motivation to change its opinions or behaviors. But is dissonance not most strong *after* a decision has been made? How, then, can a persuasive speech be concerned with a phenomenon which will occur after the speech is over? The answer is that any audience in the world is made up of people who have reached hundreds of conclusions about the things they believe and the ways they behave. In short, they have already coped with the dissonance that they originally felt upon deciding to believe or reject one thing or another. The effective persuader forces an audience to re-examine their beliefs and values, to experience again the dissonance that they once felt over deciding to believe and behave as they now do.

For instance, a middle-American audience may feel quite smug about all the financial aid they have given to the local poor. They may feel that they have exceeded in their humane responsibilities to help the less fortunate. Then along comes a Peace Corp volunteer who has just spent two years in the famine-plagued region of the Sudan. She speaks to this middle-American audience, showing graphic slides of physically wrecked bodies somehow surviving on a piece of bread a day, and she tells them that 50 cents a day from each of them could end much of this suffering. The audience begins to feel dissonance, seeing the tremendous imbalance between their blessed lives and the destitute faces on the screen. They dig into their pockets and give five, ten, even twenty dollars each in an effort to even things up, to reduce the dissonance.

Psychologically, this scenario is identical to the forces behind the "Live Aid" concert which raised over $100 million to help feed Africa's starving populations. Dissonance was created, brotherhood appealed to, and dissonance reduced by the act of giving.

This nature of example makes one wonder if dissonance is not just another word for guilt. It is not. If you feel guilty, you are likely in a state of dissonance, but not all dissonance is the result of guilt. If you decide to get engaged, would you consider the resulting dissonance guilt? Of course not. You have done nothing wrong in deciding to get engaged. The dissonance you feel is anxiety produced by your inability to take two desirable routes at once.

Such a distinction is good to keep in mind. As a would-be persuader you limit yourself if you think that creating dissonance is the same as creating guilt. In many cases, audiences can not be made to feel guilty, but they can be made to feel that they are logically inconsistent. If done well, the cognitive dissonance will pressure them to change attitudes and/or behaviors.

Many of the impactful speeches delivered on behalf of the civil rights movement in the 1960's created dissonance by stressing imbalances. Malcolm X's famous "Ballot or the Bullet" speech is one such example. In the excerpt below you can see how he highlights the inequities that blacks have had to endure for generations.

> Our mothers and fathers invested sweat and blood. Three hundred and ten years we worked in this country without a dime in return—I mean without a dime in return. You let the white man walk around here talking about how rich this country is, but you never stop to think how it got rich so quick. It got rich because you made it rich. . . . Your and my mother and father, who didn't work an eight-hour shift, but worked from "can't see" in the morning to "can't see" at night, and worked for nothing, making the white man rich, making Uncle Sam rich. . . . Not only did we give our free labor, we gave of our blood. Every time he had a call to arms, we were the first ones in uniform. We died on every battlefield the white man had. We have made a greater sacrifice than anybody who's standing up in America today. We have made a greater contribution and have collected less. Civil rights . . . means: "Give it to us now. Don't wait for next year. Give it to us yesterday, and that's not fast enough." (Rein, 1969, pp. 56–57)

Though this was a 1960's speech, it is not unfamiliar. Similar speeches have been delivered in recent years by South African blacks struggling to gain their civil rights. It is a time-honored argument. The suppressed speak of the inequities between their sacrifice and their rewards. If it is done in a convincing and credible way, dissonance results, and the audiences wait for their leaders to tell them how they might help right the wrongs.

Creating dissonance is not a thing that can be done by the numbers. It requires an artisitic touch. Malcolm X could have told his audience in a straightforward way that blacks had sacrificed work and lives for this country and deserved civil rights in return. Had he done so, he probably would not have stirred any passion for his cause. Instead, he used almost poetic language to illuminate the unfairness of the situation. He talked of work in terms of " 'can't see' in the morning until 'can't see' at night" and he talked of lives in terms of dying on "every battle field the white man ever had." Such descriptions forced his audience to see and feel the inequities in powerful ways. Once he had created such high levels of dissonance, he helped them relieve it by instructing them to demand their equal rights immediately.

Malcolm X teaches us two important things about the practical use of cognitive dissonance theory. First, it can be a powerful and effective motivation tool when used well. Second, once dissonance is created, the speaker has a responsibility to give the audience ethical ways of reducing the dissonance. This may take the form of changing attitudes or behaviors or both.

SUMMARY

Leon Festinger's theory of cognitive dissonance is an elegant theory that helps us grasp conceptually the psychological process of persuasion. Without some dissonance, there is no pressure to change attitudes or behaviors. Consequently, effective persuaders are particularly adept at creating dissonance and giving their audiences practical ways for reducing the dissonance, ways that generally assist the cause that the speaker advocates.

REFERENCES

Festinger, L. (1957). *A theory of cognitive dissonance*. Stanford: Stanford University Press.
Festinger, L. (1977). Cognitive dissonance. In E. Aronson (Ed.), *Readings about the social animal* (pp. 109–123). San Francisco: W. H. Freeman and Company.
Rein, I. J. (1969). *The relevant rhetoric*. New York: The Free Press.

Source Credibility and Persuasion

3

"Credibility" is a word that has enjoyed near constant use in the past 15 years. Ever since President Nixon was forced to resign because of the Watergate scandal, "credibility gaps" and "lost credibility" and "restored credibility" are terms which have all have been used by political analysts to discuss the fate of our presidents. Most recently, President Reagan suffered a blow to his credibility due to the Irangate fiasco. Throughout the crisis, political pollsters maintained a vigil on Reagan's weakening credibility, almost as if they were monitoring his heartbeat. When the upturn came, aides said they were happy to announce the President would have a full recovery of his credibility.

Credibility is a vital issue with corporations as well. During the oil crisis of the 1970's, Exxon and Texaco and Shell all had credibility problems since many consumers believed that the shortage had been cleverly engineered by the oil industry. After the well-publicized Tylenol poisonings it was predicted that Tylenol would never relieve another headache. The company successfully overcame one of the worst credibility problems in the history of marketing. The Chrysler Corportation, too, suffered from poor credibility. Lee Iacocca took the helm and masterminded a credibility campaign that saved the company and made it profitable again.

What we typically call "public relations problems" are generally credibility problems. When disaster strikes public personalities or companies, public relations experts are called in to shore-up weakening credibility and to lay out a plan to restore it to its original strength. Marketing itself may be the art and science of communicating and maintaining the credibility of ideas, products, people, companies, and institutions.

Why all the talk about credibility? What is it? What characteristics make a person credible? Why is it so important and so difficult to regain once it has been lost? How are credibility and persuasion related? These are complex questions, but ones that we will nonetheless attempt to answer in this chapter.

A BRIEF HISTORICAL PERSPECTIVE

Skill in persuasion was essential for the citizens of ancient Greece. In their democracy, like ours, one's place in society was often determined by his ability to speak persuasively. Had you lived at that time, you likely would have been far more advanced in the art of persuasion than you are now.

As a citizen of Athens, if you were accused of a crime, you could not hire a lawyer. You had to defend yourself. And this defense would take place before juries numbering anywhere from 200 to 500 people (Kennedy, 1979, p. 18). Conversely, if you were to accuse someone of a crime, you would have to prosecute the case yourself. As you can imagine, the courtroom spectacle made for wonderful entertainment, especially in a society without our modern forms of diversion. Citizens turned out in droves to enjoy this ancient version of "The People's Court," though the available punishments were no "prime-time" matter.

The great biologist/scientist, Aristotle, undertook a study of persuasion strategies in the courts, in the legislature, and in the popular political arena to see what made a person successfully persuasive. He put his marvel of a mind to work on an analysis of persuasion, bringing to the subject the same vigor and clarity of thought that he applied to any scientific endeavor. The result of his study was a little book that survives to this day. It is called *Rhetoric,* which, loosely translated, means "persuasion." Yet it is more than that. It might be sub-titled, "A list of all the ways that people can be persuaded." It is for this latter reason that Aristotle's *Rhetoric* is regarded by a good many experts as the most brilliant work on persuasion ever written. He systematically explained the essential elements of persuasion and how they function.

After thinking long and hard about persuasion Aristotle came to the conclusion that a person who wished to be persuasive must have a high level of *ethos.* He said that ethos, which was his term for credibility, consisted of "good sense, good character, and good will." In short, the audience must perceive the speaker as being intelligent and wise (which is demonstrated in the message), of strong moral fiber (which is demonstrated in the life and actions of the speaker), and care more about his audience than himself (which should be felt by his audience). You can easily see how Aristotle's definitions of ethos or credibility can help you assess a speaker today. Select any politician you like and rate him or her on good sense, good character, and good will. Your favorite political leader will probably rate high in all three areas.

AN ANALYSIS OF CREDIBILITY

An observation one might hear made in the study of speech communication is the following "truism:"

PEOPLE HAVE DIFFICULTY SEPARATING SOURCE AND MESSAGE.

If receivers have difficulty differentiating between perceptions of you the speaker and the speech, we have discovered an important implication for persuasive communication. The implication is that persuasive communicators must be aware of and control the effect they have on how well the audience receives and responds to their persuasive intent. The great persuasion strategist of ancient Rome, Quintillian, referred to artful persuasion as "the good man speaking well." Thus, audiences will be nonconsciously making judgments of *both* the speaker as a good person and the speech as well spoken.

In the context of the communication process, persons tend to assign value to appearance and behavior. Based upon those assigned values or judgments, they construct impressions of the actions, qualities, and attitudes of those with whom they communicate (O'Donnell & Kable, 1982). For example, once one of the authors saw a college student moving around on campus by means of a skateboard. Almost instantly, judgments were made about the student's level of maturity. As the adolescent weaved in and out of pedestrian traffic along the sidewalk, the skateboard's movement caused well-adjusted walking students to jump, jolt to a halt, and in general, to dodge the fast-moving vehicle. This person was judged to be self-concerned and unaware of the world around him as well as immature. As luck would have it, the student skated into the author's class. What an excellent opportunity this was to discuss impressions formed based on the appearance and behavior of the aimless skater. Oddly enough, the skating college student was running for office on campus, and had given no thought to how his behavior might affect the impressions he made on others.

Just as the skater needed to polish his image, so do persuaders need to give thought to how they can make their own character look right. It would be very useful, then, if the persuasive speaker could find ways to help the listener construct positive, receptive impressions so that the persuasive message intent will be accomplished.

The single, most critical variable in the success of your persuasive message is credibility. Credibility has been studied in interpersonal, organizational, and public communication contexts. In fact, "there has probably been more research on the effects of credibility on communication than on any other single variable in communication process (McCroskey & Wheeless, 1978, p. 101)."

Credibility may be defined as a multidimensional perception of trust, belief, and/or confidence. We have offered, so far in this chapter, a rather lengthy introduction to the concept of credibility. If our reason for so doing is not yet clear, let us make it so: IF YOU CANNOT PRESENT YOURSELF AS A CREDIBLE SOURCE, NOTHING YOU CAN SAY WILL MAKE YOU PERSUASIVE. To put it another way, the more credible you can be as a speaker, the more likely it is that your speech will be believed. You may have already deduced that a credible message may enhance receivers' confidence in the source. A source, a message, or a channel may elicit perceptions of credibility. However, our primary focus will be on source credibility, and the factors you can use to enhance that source credibility.

Source credibility has been studied in a number of different ways. We know from these studies that receptivity to communication is increased as credibility increases (Scott & Powers, 1978). Perceived credibility of an immediate supervisor increases job satisfaction (Falcione, 1974a), and participation in decision-making (Falcione, 1974b). A credible teacher evokes more information-seeking by students (Hurt, Scott, & McCroskey, 1978). Most important for us as persuasive speakers is the fact that credibility absolutely must be high in the minds of our listeners. Aristotle called credibility the most critical element of proof. His assessment has not been widely disputed.

When the authors were in graduate school together, we wanted to test this assumption for ourselves. Having nothing else to do we conducted a study of source credibility. We constructed a persuasive message on the danger of nuclear power generation. The message was printed as a quotation and attributed to various news sources. With eight groups of student subjects, we told each group that a different source had provided the anti-nuclear power message. Group one was told the message had first appeared in *Playboy Magazine*. Group two was told the message came from *U.S. News and World Report*. Group three saw the same message attributed to *Reader's Digest*. Group four was told the message came from the local campus newspaper. Group five was told the message came from the *Washington Post*. For group six, the message was attributed to *The National Enquirer*. Group seven was given the message and no source was assigned. Group eight heard the message recorded in stereo on audiotape, and was told the source was NBC Radio News.

In this study, several things were measured, most notably attitude change and source credibility. In terms of average credibility rankings from high to low, the sources were rated in this order:

The Washington Post
U.S. News and World Report
NBC Radio News
Playboy
Reader's Digest
No Source
The National Enquirer
The local college newspaper.

There was clearly a relationship between source credibility and attitude change. In other words, the *Washington Post* and *U.S. News and World Report* caused a greater attitude change than other sources in the direction of the message (intensified opposition to nuclear power). On the other hand, low credibility sources seem to have a "boomerang effect." That is, in the case of *The National Enquirer,* students changed their opinion in the Opposite direction of the message, or became more strongly *in favor* of nuclear power. Perhaps, then, a source can have "negative credibility," which tends to make receivers believe the opposite of the persuasive message.

The above study confirmed the obvious for us: credibility of source enhances the possibility of attitude change. *The National Enquirer* boomerang effect confirmed what other sources have noted about low credibility. If a sender "is perceived as low in credibility, we are likely to misperceive the messages that the communicator gives us; we are less likely to expose ourselves to that person ['s messages]; we are less likely to learn from that person; and we are less likely to be influenced by that person (McCroskey & Wheeless, 1976, p. 106)."

Components of Credibility

We said that credibility is a multidimensional construct. What that means is that there are many elements which combine to make up credibility. Depending upon which scholar you read, you might find credibility to be described as consisting of competence, trustworthiness, attractiveness, and charisma, to mention a few (cf. Brooks, 1978; Emmert & Donaghy, 1981). Aristotle's three components in *The Rhetoric* were good character, good will, and good sense (sagacity). The most commonly used model in empirical research on credibility is based on the work of McCroskey (McCroskey, Holdridge, & Toomb, 1974; McCroskey, Jenson, & Valencia, 1973). This model described credibility as having at least the five dimensions outlined below.

COMPETENCE—the degree to which a person is perceived to be an expert on or have knowledge of the subject matter being communicated.

CHARACTER—the degree to which a source is perceived as a reliable, essentially good and trustworthy message source.

COMPOSURE—the degree to which the source is perceived as able to maintain control over emotions.

EXTROVERSION—the degree to which the source is perceived as talkative, bold, outgoing, and dynamic.

SOCIABILITY—the degree to which the audience perceives the source as one with whom they *could* be friends.

The power of credibility was demonstrated powerfully through the use of this five dimensional model in another study we conducted. This second study was a political communication assessment of the credibility of candidate Ronald Reagan during the 1980 presidential campaign. Actually, two studies were conducted. The first study dealt with the credibility of candidate Ronald Reagan based upon a four minute advertising spot, and the second study involved a credibility comparison of Reagan versus Carter during the televised debates for the 1980 presidential race. The results of our research were so interesting that Peter Dailey, Reagan's Media Strategist during the 1980 campaign, asked us to share the data with him, as well as our thoughts about the implications of the data.

The Advertising Study

In examining candidate Ronald Reagan's source credibility, we administered the scale which would measure perceptions of Reagan on the five dimensions of credibility (competence, character, sociability, composure, and extroversion). Following the administration of the credibility scales, we showed subjects a four minute, twenty second advertising spot, featuring Ronald Reagan speaking to the television viewer in that warm and interpersonal style that has become his trademark. He talked about the poor economy and the ways that we could make America "stand tall" again. Following the ad, we administered the credibility scales again. The ad improved Reagan's ratings on all five dimensions of credibility. Three of the five increases were statistically significant: competence, character, and extroversion. There was also a shift in favor of Ronald Reagan as a candidate for president. Most interesting were the responses to open questions on the second scale. The students who found Reagan highly credible, when asked why they supported him, used Reagan's very words as spoken in the ad. The point is that the message not only elicited perceptions of credibility, but the message was such that the students quoted passages as if they were gospel.

The Debate Study

The 1980 presidential debates were the source of further credibility study. In this research, subjects were asked to rate Reagan and Carter on the five dimensions of credibility before and after the debate. Each candidate increased perceptions of credibility for certain dimensions. Changes were analyzed and final credibility ratings were compared. Following the debates, Carter increased ratings slightly on competence and extroversion, while he actually decreased his ratings on sociability. Reagan, on the other hand, increased perceptions of competence, character, sociability, and extroversion. Comparisons of post-debate credibility showed Reagan significantly higher than Carter on competence, composure, sociability, and extroversion. Following the debates, about 68% of the subjects indicated that they favored Reagan, which was an exact representation of the voting pattern for that county in Texas. It is interesting that a candidate could evoke higher credibility perceptions than a president, particularly on competence. However, the results demonstrate the critical value of communicating one's credibility along with what one is saying in his or her persuasive message. Reagan's landslide victory is due in part to his skillful communication of his credibility.

A Final Thought on Components

It would seem at first glance that knowing these five dimensions would make it very easy to establish credibility. For example, to establish perceptions of competence, the speaker would make a concerted effort to introduce elements into the message which would enhance perceptions of competence (Emmert & Donaghy, 1981). Certainly, you would want to do just that, but you should be aware that the complexity of the communication process makes establishing credibility a bit more complicated than it seems. For this reason, we will discuss further the perceptual attribution process before we start thinking about how to generate perceptions of credibility in your receivers.

Source credibility is something established *in process*. Since a process is ongoing and complex, we should begin to see how difficult establishing credibility can be. Credibility is in part attributed to us because of how attractive we are perceived to be and what we are preceived to have in common with receivers (O'Donnell & Kable, 1982).

Much of anyone's perceived credibility is based upon observed characteristics. Included in observed characteristics would be such items as a person's reputation and nonverbal communication. Observed nonverbal characteristics include both those things we cannot control, such as our own stature; and those things we can control, such as dress and grooming, gesture, facial expression, posture, distance, and eye gaze. Observed verbal characteristics may also contribute to perceptions of credibility. Our choice of words and adherence to norms (such as controlling obscene language) may affect credibility (O'Donnell & Kable, 1982). It is also true that we may reveal some of ourselves, and those revelations may impact credibility. Such things as our humor, use of examples, commitment to persuasive goals, age, education, and experience may enhance credibility (Brooks, 1978; O'Donnell & Kable, 1982). There may also be a credibility transfer if we associate ourselves with credible people or quote credible sources of information. Just as there is guilt by association, so is there credibility by association.

THREE STAGES OF CREDIBILITY

Finally, we might examine credibility factors in human interaction in terms of stages. Basically, credibility is "granted" to a source in three stages. First, there is *external* credibility, or the reputation that precedes the speaker. Second is the *internal* credibility, or that which the speaker establishes during the speech. Third is the *ending* credibility, which results from the interaction of external and internal credibility.

External Credibility

External credibility is what the audience knows of the speaker prior to the speech. Most visiting lecturers to college campuses are invited on the basis of their external credibility. John Kenneth Galbraith would be invited because of his work in economics. Desmond Tutu would be invited because of his work in South Africa and for being a winner of the Nobel Peace Prize. Gary Larson would be invited on the strength of his cartoons and obvious human insights. If the audience is unaware of a speaker's external credibility, then it is up to the introducer to make them aware. More than anything else, the job of an introducer is to build the credibility of the featured speaker, to say, "Here's why you should listen to this person." If the speaker's external credibility is already well known by everyone in the audience, then the introducer tends to fall victim to the old cliche: "Our speaker tonight needs no introduction." Then, inevitably of course, he or she goes right ahead and introduces the speaker anyway.

External credibility is comprised of accomplishments worthy of note. Your resume is a document designed to build your external credibility. Diplomas in doctors' offices aid their external credibility and our peace of mind. Similarly, speakers who have written books, obtained prestigious degrees, held important positions in society, traveled to places few people have ever been, conquered enormous odds, or made earth-shattering discoveries all are high in external credibility, providing that the audience knows of such accomplishments prior to the speech. Such external credibility increases their persuasive power.

Internal Credibility

Internal credibility is established within the speech itself. Suppose we attended a lecture by a Dr. Janice Smith on the need for nuclear disarmament. Now, prior to the speech we have never heard a thing about Dr. Smith. She is a nobody to us and has only the credibility that being a "featured speaker" can give her. Other than that, she has to "prove" herself to us. This she can do in the speech itself. She may demonstrate tremendous fluency in nuclear armament jargon (she knows the words so she must know the subject). She may cite ten or twenty rare documents that she has personally studied (she has exclusive knowledge). She may mention occasions on which she has discussed nuclear disarmament face-to-face with world leaders (credibility by association). Providing that we believe her claims, then the good Dr. Smith will benefit from a high level of internal credibility.

Since most students are low in external credibility, they have to focus on establishing internal credibility. This is accomplished by transferring the external credibility of others to yourself. You may not be perceived as an economics expert, but when you quote Galbraith, people will likely find you more believable. You are using Galbraith's external credibility to strenghten your internal credibility. After you have cited a good number of sources, then the audience begins to see that you have "read the books" and will therefore allow you to make a few assertions with minimal support. You have established a kind of credit. In other words, when you use credibility transference enough, after a while, some of that begins to rub off on you and you are left with some external credibility yourself.

After years of studying persuasion, one of the most important principles that we have learned is this: IT ISN'T WHAT YOU SAY, IT'S WHO YOU GET TO SAY IT. Students approach us frequently wanting to know the golden argument to present to their parents that will get their parents to let them go to school in Europe or get their parents to buy them a new car or pay for half of their tuition. We tell them that their problem is not in their argument, it's in the source of the argument. They must do as they have always done, get the right person to intercede on their behalf, to argue their case for them or to allow them to say that that credible person supports the idea. So the solution to their problem is not in *what* they will say but in *who* they will get to say it.

The same principle holds true for establishing an effective level of internal credibility. Give thought to *who* will be a credible source to your audience and use their credibility to boost your own persuasive power. It isn't what you say, it's who you get to say it, or who you get to join you in saying it that matters most in persuasion.

Ending Credibility

This results from the interaction between external and internal credibility. After the speech is over, the audience goes home with an adjusted assessment of the speaker's credibility. This can be more positive or more negative than the level of credibility originally ascribed. In the case of Dr. Smith, since her internal credibility was strong, we would leave the lecture with a much more credible assessment of her than when we came.

Credibility is a perception. It is not some amount of "good" that a person owns. It is granted by the audience and it can be taken away at any time. Since credibility is a perception, there are many technically illogical uses of it, but still, highly effective uses. For instance, sometimes perceptions of *doctorness* are more persuasive than actual doctor-endorsements. If this were not true, then Cliff from "All My Kids" could not successfully recommend a medicine by saying, "I'm not a doctor, but a play one on TV. . . ." If you will remember this, then you will remember that *being* credible is not enough. You must be *perceived* as credible, too.

ESTABLISHING CREDIBILITY AS A PERSUADER

Based upon the research in this field and dozens of communication texts, we might offer any number of guidelines to you as ways of enhancing perceptions of credibility. You must bear in mind that what is credible to one receiver may not be credible to another. For example, a man in a three-piece suit might be seen as credible by a white-collar audience but that same attire might hinder his credibility with another audience. Obviously, the better your audience analysis, the easier it will be for you to build your credibility. In general, the guidelines below will improve your odds of being perceived as a credible speaker.

Present a neat, well-groomed appearance.

Be well prepared (rehearsed) for your presentation.

Establish eye contact with your audience from the first word of your speech, and continue scanning the audience throughout the speech.

Demonstrate a rational, well-researched point of view, using credible sources.

Use examples with which the audience can identify, and which support your view.

Demonstrate your personal commitment to your persuasive intent in your words and in terms of a dynamic delivery.

Use humor when appropriate.

Use gestures and facial expressions to reinforce meaning.

Cite any expertness you have on the subject, but do so without giving the appearance of bragging.

Speak loudly enough to be heard, but not too loudly.

Do not be overly dependent on notes.

Use intense and emotional language sparingly.

Vary your voice's pitch and rate to communicate.

Articulate clearly, but use a conversational style.

In general, try to convey an enthusiastic, intelligent, mature, and confident self.

Seems fairly easy, doesn't it? You can do it, can't you? We knew you could!

SUMMARY

The more you can do to enhance your credibility, the better your odds of succeeding at your persuasive intent. Credibility is a complex perception attributed to each person based on a variety of factors ranging from those over which you have a lot of control to those you cannot control at all. You should bear in mind that the way you present your self and your message will in large measure determine not only whether you succeed in persuasion class, but in life itself.

REFERENCES

Brooks, W. D. (1978) *Speech communication* (3rd ed.). Dubuque, Ia: William C. Brown.

Emmert, P. & Donaghy, W. C. (1981) *Human communication: elements and contexts.* Reading, Ma: Addison-Wesley Publishing Co.

Falcione, R. L. (1974a) Communication climate and satisfaction with immediate supervision. *Journal of Applied Communication Research* (2) 13–20.

Falcione, R. L. (1974b) Credibility: qualifier of subordinate participation. *Journal of Business Communication* (11) pp. 43–54.

Kennedy, G. (1979) *Classical rhetoric: its christian and secular tradition from ancient to modern times.* Chapel Hill, North Carolina: The Chapel Hill Press.

Hurt, H. T., Scott, M. & McCroskey, J. C. (1978) *Communication in the classroom.* Reading, Ma: Addison-Wesley Publishing Co.

McCroskey, J. C., Holdridge, W. E. & Tomb, J. D. (1974) An instrument for measuring the source credibility of basic speech communication instructors. *The Speech Teacher* (23) pp. 26–33.

McCroskey, J. C., Jenson, L. & Valencia, C. (1973) Measures of credibilityof peers and spouses. Paper presented at the annual meeting of the International Communication Association, Montreal.

McCroskey, J. C. & Wheeless, L. R. (1976) *Introduction to Human Communication.* Boston: Allyn & Bacon, Inc.

O'Donnell, V. & Kable J. (1982) *Persuasion: An Interactive Dependency Approach.* New York: Random House.

Scott, M. D. & Powers, W. G. (1978) *Interpersonal Communication: A Question of Needs.* Boston: Houghton Mifflin Company.

Topic Selection and Audience Analysis

4

"I don't have anything to talk about" is the most frequent complaint we hear from students taking performance courses in speech. This problem, which is assuredly a real one, is one of the greatest differences between college and professional life. After you have completed your degree and are working in your chosen field, you will be asked to lend your expertise to many causes. In such cases, your topic will be given to you by the group or organization asking you to speak. If you are a nuclear engineer, you will undoubtedly be asked to speak on the safety or dangers of nuclear power generation. The problem of topic selection for the professional is more a problem of narrowing the scope of the talk than finding a topic. We realize that this observation does not help those of you who currently have "nothing to say." In truth, you have a great deal to say, you simply need ways of becoming sensitive to your own views. We are going to provide you with some techniques for identifying and clarifying your views so that you can select topics for which you have some passion. This is very important. In informational speaking, you should at least *like* your topic; to be at your best in persuasive speaking, you should *love* your topic. Afterall, have you ever heard a truly persuasive speaker who was not a passionate supporter of his or her point of view. Did Martin Luther King just "like" the idea of civil rights? Was Bob Geldof (the organizer of the Live Aid concerts) merely supportive of the need to feed Ethiopia's starving? Does Billy Graham think that accepting Christ is something that we should all get around to doing someday?

Admittedly, we cannot all be possessed with a mission. Still there are dozens of things about which we have strong feelings. These "things" make good topics for persuasive speeches. The questions that follow are designed to help you discover or rediscover attitudes and beliefs and values that are important to you. From these areas you should be able to select a thesis around which you can construct a persuasive speech.

TOPIC SELECTION

What makes you angry?

When is the last time you really got mad? What were you mad about? An unfair exam? A speeding ticket? Ridiculous registration procedures? A fight with your boyfriend or girlfriend or spouse? When is the last time you said, "What I wish people could understand is - - -?" What were you referring to? This line of questioning can lead to your deepest feelings about the world around you. Many high-quality classroom speeches have sprung from this line of self-inquiry. A student who was genuinely angry about what he perceived to be an unfair testing practice in his persuasion class used his anger productively. He persuaded his classmates to join him in protesting the unfairness and was successful in affecting a change in testing policy. Another student who was tired of constantly defending his fraternity against stereotypical attacks did what he could to dispel that stereotypical image. He convinced his audience that the "Animal House" image of fraternities blinded the public to the many good things that they do in the local community. A young woman upset by the excessive litter on campus did something about it: she persuaded her classmates to join her for a Saturday morning of campus cleaning. Find what makes you angry and you have tapped into a plentiful source of persuasive speech topics.

What jobs have you had in recent years?

If you are like most students you have worked in a part-time or seasonal job recently. This experience has probably given you the benefit of some unique insight into social, government, or business issues. A student who has spent a summer working for a clothing store might convince her audience that Guess jeans are truly the best buy in the jeans market. A former grocery stocker could speak on the wisdom of buying generic products. Those with experience in fast-food restaurants could reinforce our allegiance to McDonald's or Burger King or Wendy's, or they could convince us to "MacBreak" (sorry) our fast-food habits for good.

Topics culled from job experience are good for two reasons: You have credibility on the subject and likely you have already presented your major arguments to friends. In short, you have been composing your speech for a long time.

What current social and political events interest you?

Too often students say that they don't know anything about politics or current events because they spend so much time studying that news gets to them three days after the fact. We recognize that college can be a terribly insulating environment against current, hard news. Nonetheless, the more significant issues do manage to seep through the ivory towers. They seep through in the form of campus demonstrations, special lectures, classroom discussions, and letters to the editor in the school newspaper. Perhaps focusing on what does get through is a good idea because it tells you what the student population (your audience) has on its mind. Is the fear of Aids prevalent on your campus? Then a persuasive speech on the need for "safe sex" might be in order. Have there been demonstrations against C.I.A. agents interviewing on campus? A speech defending their rights to be there would be interesting. Has a prominent speaker come to your campus to solicit support for the Contra-rebels in Nicaragua? You might prepare a speech that would serve as a rebuttal to that position.

What popular magazines do you read regularly?

Magazines from *Atlantic Monthly* to *Sports Illustrated* to *Playboy* are rife with potential persuasive speech topics. Moreover, topics culled from popular magazines generally are on the cutting edge of society's concerns. Hence, they are less likely to be "worn out," as are the ever-popular abortion, capital punishment, and seat-belt topics. In *Atlantic Monthly,* one will find discussion on the constitutionality of drug-testing. In *Sports Illustrated,* the playoff system for college football is often attacked or supported. *Playboy,* despite the old joke inferring the opposite, does contain articles by some of the best minds in the country writing on controversial subjects ranging from censorship to the ethics of corporate takeovers.

If you are so swamped with required readings for your classes that pleasure reading is out, you can at least stroll by a news stand. Here, just reading the teasers on the covers of magazines can provide you with 1001 ideas for persuasive speech topics.

What have you learned in your major area of study that has convinced you to change some long-standing belief or opinion?

Education, by definition, should challenge ignorance. Consequently, no matter what your major is, you will find that your values and beliefs are constantly in a state of flux. Economics majors are taught to see the world as a complex set of interactions wherein every new economic policy causes a reaction somewhere else in the economy. Hence, students studying in this area might try to convince their classmates to "see" the world as they have been taught to "see" it. A major in Agriculture may have special insight into the health benefits of eating the beef produced by the new strain of lean cattle. Parks and Recreation majors might attempt to prove that certain hunting programs within the national parks are indeed helpful to conservationist goals.

As is the case with work-related topics, speaking within the area of your major gives you credibility and confidence. Likely you know and care about the topic and no doubt you have heard all of the important issues discussed in your classes.

Should all of these brainstorming questions fail you, have heart. We have included in Appendix A of this book, a list that, as Ed McMahon would say, "includes everything in the world you could possibly want to know about persuasive speech topics." Turn to that section and help yourself.

Refining the Topic

We believe that there is no such thing as an improper topic; there is only improper treatment of topics. True, some topics appear improper on the surface, such as speaking to the American Bar Association about the need to limit jury awards in liability suits. That does not mean that it should be dismissed as a topic, however. There are ways of speaking the unspeakable. You must be creative in finding the angle that will make that audience listen. Thus, it is not the topic, but rather, what you do with it that counts.

Once you have settled on a subject area, you must make some effort to narrow the scope of treatment so that it can be handled within the allotted time. Not only will this make your speech preparation easier, it will probably make your speech more persuasive. Instead of delivering a speech that is in favor of capital punishment, why not speak on a sub-topic of capital punishment. Support the "insane but guilty" verdict. Support capital punishment in cases of multiple deaths. Argue that the phrase "cruel and unusual punishment" has long been misinterpreted. Generally, the more specific you can get, the more likely your audience will be learning something new and the more likely they will find your speech interesting and credible.

As soon as possible in the speech development process, you should write out your specific purpose or thesis statement. Write it in large letters on a note card:

TO PERSUADE MY AUDIENCE THAT THE WAR ON DRUGS IS MORE HYPE THAN SUBSTANCE

TO CONVINCE MY AUDIENCE THAT THE NISSAN 300ZX IS THE BEST SPORTS CAR IN THE RANGE OF $18,000 TO $20,000

TO PERSUADE MY AUDIENCE TO JOIN ME IN TAKING CHRISTMAS BASKETS TO THE POOR

TO CONVINCE MY AUDIENCE THAT JESSE JACKSON IS THE BEST CANDIDATE FOR PRESIDENT

The reason for writing out your thesis so early is so that you will always know where you are going and what you are trying to accomplish. Many speeches fail because neither the audience nor the speaker knows what the aim of the speech is. Everyone is left confused. When you have your goal firmly in mind early on, then the entire development of your speech will work toward that realization. As David Belasco, the great Broadway producer once remarked, "If you can't write your idea on the back of my calling card, you don't have a clear idea." Writing out your thesis statement helps you make sure that you have a clear idea.

AUDIENCE ANALYSIS

As teachers of persuasion we are from time to time asked this provocative question: "What qualities make for the most persuasive speaker of all?" Our answer never varies. We answer with a question: "For what audience?" You may think that this is a cop-out of sorts, but it really isn't. We cannot answer the question honestly without knowing the audience that the hypothetical "most persuasive speaker" will address. The qualities that make a speaker persuasive vary from audience to audience, which is why we are going to spend considerable time on audience analysis.

The more you know about your audience, the greater are your chances of achieving your persuasive goals. Over and over during the research and preparation phases of your speech you should ask the question, "Who is my audience?" Consideration of the audience ought to dictate topic treatment, organizational structure, and even the type of evidence used in the speech.

There is an old saying among journalists: "Readers write newspapers." We might extend this to say also that "movie goers create films," "voters design political campaigns" and "audiences compose speeches." Newspapers must adapt to the collective desires of their readers or go out of business. Without the success of the original "Friday the 13th," what Roger Ebert calls the prototype for "dead teenager movies," we would have never had enough sequels to have a "Friday the 13th Film Festival." Speakers who fail to adapt their messages to the psychological and sociological needs of their audience will not succeed in accomplishing their persuasive intent. Show us a case of unsuccessful persuasion, and, most of the time, we will show you a case of poor audience analysis.

Suppose that you have been asked to deliver a persuasive speech. You have been given a topic and you now need to know about the audience. What do you want to know about them? What will the resulting information tell you in terms of how you should prepare your speech?

Demographics

First of all, you want all the demographic information you can get your hands on. Demographics are data that give you a composite picture of the audience, data that include such things as age, sex, education level, income, occupation and religion. It is from demographics that we have gained such wonderful new terms as Yuppies (young urban professionals) and Buppies (black urban professionals) and Dinks (Double income, no kids). Every successful publication and television program in this country has elaborate knowledge of its demographics. Without such data, they could not persuade their audiences to continue subscribing or watching. *Redbook* knows that its audience consists mainly of "young mothers between the ages of 25 and 44" and that over half of their "readers work outside the home and have children under 18" (Williams, 1987, p. 662). *Mademoiselle* is written for "college-educated, unmarried working women 18–34" (Williams, 1987, p. 660). We cannot overstress the value of knowing everything possible about your audience. If you want a secret of persuasion, that is it. The answers to most persuasive problems are are in the audience. All you have to do is ask them the right questions and they will tell you what arguments will persuade them and how those arguments should be presented. Some of the great slogans in advertising history have come right out of the consumer audience. "When you're out of Schlitz, you're out of beer" was first said by a man who was drinking Schlitz in a bar. It was made famous by the advertising executive who overheard him.

Even rock bands must continually listen to their audiences in order to adapt to their wishes and stay popular. Dire Straits was once in a TV store that had an entire bank of televisions tuned to MTV. They happened to see one of the workers there nudge his buddy, point to the rock band on the television screens, and say "That ain't workin'! That's easy money!" Out of that sentiment, as you probably know, came the smash-hit "Money for Nothing." Clearly, listening carefully to your audience can be a lucrative investment of time.

The speaker, too, needs to know as much as possible about the demographics of the audience. The vital element of the demographics will vary according to the persuasive goal. Sometimes age will be more important than sex and sometimes occupation will matter more than religion. It will be most helpful, for the purpose of understanding the strategic power of demographics, if we consider each element independently.

Age

Aristotle, who was a pioneer in so many disciplines, was a pioneer in persuasion as well. He was one of the first theorists to systematically examine the effects of age on thought and action. Though he wrote the following over 2300 years ago, it still has merit today:

> Young men are lustful in character, and apt to do what they lust after. Of the bodily desires, they are most apt to indulge, and to exceed in, the sexual. They are changeable and fickle in their desires, which are violent but soon appeased; for their impulses are rather keen than great, like the hunger and thirst of the sick. They are passionate, quick to anger and apt to obey their impulse; and they are under the dominion of their passion, for, by reason of ambition, they cannot bear to be slighted, and they are indignant, if they think they are wronged—They are credulous, because, as yet, they have not been deceived. They are sanguine, because they are heated, as with wine, and also because they have not had many disappointments. They live for most part by hope; for hope is of the future, as memory of the past, and for young men, the future is long and the past short; since, on the first day of life, there is nothing to remember and everything to hope. (Jedd, 1909, p. 99)

In this modern world of mass media, age is still the greatest single factor in determining the content of messages. Saturday morning television is for children and the programs and the advertisers interact in clever ways to appeal to childish impulses. Parents have even organized to combat the unbelievable success advertisers have had in using demographic and psychographic data to influence their children.

For the speaker, the age of the audience determines the examples that will be used, the data that will be displayed, the style of humor that may be included, the language that will be chosen, and even the clothes the speaker will wear.

The speaker who is substantially older or younger than the audience has to work hard to overcome the age gap. The young person addressing an older crowd must demonstrate a knowledge of history or risk being judged "shallow" or "naive." When John F. Kennedy ran for the presidency, he frequently demonstrated a broad and deep knowledge of history and world affairs. This helped him overcome criticism that he was too young to be president. Conversely, an older speaker addressing a younger audience must show that he has knowledge of their modern struggles or risk being regarded as "behind the times" or "out of touch."

Sex

The male-female ratio of an audience always impacts what can and cannot be said. Obviously, there are things that can be said to an all female audience that will serve to unify them whereas the same thing said in a mixed audience will only alienate one part of the audience from the other. Comedians struggle with the audience mix problem. Mark Twain said that the women of his time had a sobering effect on the men in the audience. Men, he said, would never allow themselves to fully enjoy good humor in the presence of women (Lorch, 1968, p. 239). Likely, the same could be said about women in the presence of men. Neither sex is ever as free in the presence of the other as they are on their own. If a group of teen-age women are watching television and a tampon ad comes on, they are not bothered by it. Add one male to the group and both sexes will be a little embarrassed.

If a female speaker is addressing an all female audience she can rely heavily on examples pulled from the female experience. Her use of language can be more vivid on some subjects than it could be in a mixed audience. Naturally, the same is true for a man addressing an all male audience. But this is the easy part. Speaking to your own sex is as easy as speaking to people your own age. What about the case of a woman speaking to an all male audience or a man speaking to an all female audience? The prudent strategy in such a case is to violate expectancies to some extent. Don't allow yourself to fall into the stereotypical patterns that they might expect of you. A woman might use a few sports metaphors or examples to illustrate her arguments whereas a man might use a few quotations from women that most women like and respect, such as Gloria Steinham, Sandra Day O'Conner, or even Erma Bombeck and Joan Rivers for the humorous touch. This must be done in sincerety and moderation, however. Excess in this regard reeks of false-praise and ingratiation.

Handling the mixed audience is a little less difficult since this is what most of us are used to. Since a young age we have learned how to adapt messages so that they can be communicated to both sexes simultaneously. Most of what we do is to focus on things that both sexes have in common such as the fact that we are all human and value life and love. Persuasive speakers must concentrate on the things that the audience shares which will negate the effects of the male-female split. If the audience is composed mainly of Californians or stock-brokers or Catholics, then we know what to stress to encourage audience cohesion. In a one sex audience, sex is likely the most important common factor and should be used to its full persuasive potential. In the case of a mixed audience, one should appeal to those demographic elements that transcend sexual differences and serve to unify the group.

Religion

Religious convictions run deep in most people's value systems. Being sensitive or insensitive to such convictions can mean the difference between resounding success and embarrassing failure for the persuasive speaker. Virtually all major elections held in this country result in at least one candidate damaging his or her campaign by making remarks that are taken to be anti-Semitic, anti-Catholic, or anti-religious in general. Once this nature of faux pas is made, it is practically impossible for the candidate to regain credibility with those who have been insulted. "I'm sorry" just won't do it. The voters may even believe that the candidate is sorry, but they cannot help but believe that the prejudice is deep-seated.

Religion is a volatile dimension of demographics. It is a powerful force if ably directed, but it has such explosive potential that only those speakers who know what they are doing should incorporate it into a persuasive strategy. If you are not Jewish but addressing a Jewish audience, then it is best to tred lightly on Jewish issues. Otherwise, you could deeply offend your entire audience without ever knowing exactly how you managed to do it. Still, if you think that you must anchor into Jewish doctrine in order to sell your program, then find several Jewish friends who will help you structure your message so that it will not offend anyone and so that it will have the power that you want it to have. If you have no Jewish friends, then make some prior to making your speech.

Most of the time, however, we are faced with audiences that are of mixed religious persuasions. Customarily, we move away from individual faiths and appeal to a kind of generic religion. This is the religion that we share at sporting events and in pledges and oaths, and the religion that the president relies on in his speeches. Professor Rod Hart calls this our "civil religion." He says that "even the novice student of American history is well aware of the pains the American people have taken to surround their political sayings with things divine" (Hart, 1977, p. 13). He points out that from the days of the Mayflower Compact to our present day use of "In God We Trust" on our coins, we Americans have always had a civil religion that has bonded us despite our individual faiths. Hart illustrates:

> [We have] insisted that our presidents take their oaths of office on the Bible, established Capitol prayer rooms, proclaimed national days of prayer, brandished federal banners in our churches, and talked, talked, talked—of God's special love for America, of America's unique responsibility to God, of a New Israel and a Chosen People, of rededicating ourselves to the principles of basic Christian Americanism, and so on. (Hart, 1977, p. 12)

When needing to rely on religion as a primary means of motivating a mixed religious audience, it is best to rely on our "civil religion" so as not to offend nor alienate the different religious factions represented.

Race

Race, like religion, can be either an incredibly effective tool for the persuasive speaker or a disaster about to happen. If a white speaker addresses a predominantly black audience, some knowledge about black history and leaders ought to be shown. A gratuitous mentioning of Martin Luther King, Jr. is not the answer. The speaker should go beyond what is normal for white speakers. The audience will be surprised if a white speaker quotes Frederick Douglass, Booker T. Washington, W. E. B. Dubois or Malcolm X. Just the fact that the speaker has bothered to become acquainted with these great figures will please the audience, and if the speaker is seen to be sincere, the audience will perceive him or her as more credible than they would have otherwise.

Another thing that the white speaker addressing a black audience would want to do is to be more animated in delivery style. Most black audiences find white speakers boring because they are, by comparison, monotone, stiff and formal. This is not to say that the white speaker should attempt to take on a black style, which would be comical at best, and racist at worst, but to be more animated within the limits of his or her own style of speech.

The black speaker addressing the white audience does not have to make a reciprocal adjustment. Afterall, white audiences frequently find that they, too, like the black style of oratory better than the white style.

We have endeavored to take you through the major demographic elements, the ones that cause the greatest trouble for speakers. The other elements such as occupation, education, and income, can be analyzed in a way similar to the way we have examined age, sex, religion, and race. Keep in mind, of course, that audiences rarely come in such neat packages. Not often do we get an audience of Catholic priests between the ages of 30 and 35 who were all raised in New York City. Most of the time we get audiences that are sixty percent one sex or another, raised in all parts of the country, of 15 different religions, from poor to filthy rich, 40% Democrat, 30% Republican, 20% Independent and 5% Reactionary, not to mention ranging in age from 18 to 88. We don't call America the melting pot for nothing! So we must always search out the greatest common factor in the audience, and the greatest common factor may be that they are an audience, in the same place at the same time surviving the same day and coping with the same weather. Find out what the common demographic elements are and use them.

Incidentally, this is one area in which you "have it made" as far as classroom speaking is concerned. Never again are you likely to have an audience that is so much like you—young, allegedly educated, and poor. And not only that. Your audience may be one of the most understanding you will ever have, since they all have to give speeches too. Use all these things to your advantage, from topic selection and narrowing, to planning persuasive strategy. Don't make the mistake of thinking of your classmates as a "mock" audience. They are just as real as you are. They can be influenced and convinced and inspired just like any other audience in the world. So get out there as a real human being talking to other real human beings.

Psychographics

It used to be that speakers were forced to rely on a "good guess" when it came to assessing audience attitudes and beliefs and values in relation to the purpose of the speech. Admittedly, the "best guess" is still the audience analysis method that is used most. However, you should be aware that many political speakers, as well as business leaders, are now regularly gathering psychographic data on audiences prior to the day of their speeches.

Psychographic information helps us get inside the heads of the audience to assess their collective attitudes and beliefs, and the strengths and weaknesses of those attitudes and beliefs, in relation to our persuasive goal. Without gathering such data, then we may tend to create a speech that is trying to solve a problem that either does not exist or is not as serious as we suspected. In short, we may end up trying to cure cancer when the audience only has a cold.

Perhaps the most common fault of all of us is what psychologists call projection—assuming that others see the world as we do and believe as we believe. In fact, it is rare for people to believe the "same" things, even about mother and apple pie. So we need some check on reality. One way to do this is to borrow some scientific methods in order to check up on collective audience realities.

There are many kinds of survey instruments that are typically used for gathering psychographic data. We will discuss two of the more commonly used instruments, the Likert-scale and the semantic differential.

The Likert-Scale

This is the scale that you are probably most familiar with. It is the scale that is used most frequently on teacher evaluation forms and on personality profile tests. Generally, the respondent is asked to read a series of statements and carefully and honestly circle the response that most accurately describes feelings about each statement. Choices often include Strongly Agree, Agree, Undecided, Disagree, and Strongly Disagree. Below are some examples of how the Likert scale might be used.

Bruce Springsteen is the top rock & roller of the 1980's.

Strongly Agree　　　*Agree*　　　*Undecided*　　　*Disagree*　　　*Strongly Disagree*

Breathing second-hand cigarette smoke can cause cancer.

Strongly Agree　　　*Agree*　　　*Undecided*　　　*Disagree*　　　*Strongly Disagree*

The modern college student is more concerned about material success than were the students of the 1970's.

Strongly Agree　　　*Agree*　　　*Undecided*　　　*Disagree*　　　*Strongly Disagree*

When designing your own survey instrument, make sure that you do not use Likert-scales for asking questions. Likerts should be used only for statements with which people are asked to agree or disagree. Additionally, be careful that you do not require your subjects to respond to more than one issue per statement. In other words, to write, "The Soviet leaders are unscrupulous and should not be bargained with," is a bad Likert statement because it asks your subjects to respond to both your characterization of the Soviet leaders as an "unscrupulous" lot and to your suggestion that they ought "not to be bargained with." One can easily agree that they are unscrupulous but still think that we should try to bargain with them, albeit carefully.

When you collect your survey instruments, each item should be numerically coded so that the verbal reponses can be translated into mathematical ones. This is done by assigning a (1) to Strongly Agree, a (2) to Agree, a (3) to Undecided, a (4) to Disagree, and a (5) to Strongly Disagree. In this way, you can add up the total reponses for each statement and divide by the number of responses to get an average attitude or belief for the entire audience. Thus, if your audience already believes strongly that second-hand cigarette smoke can cause cancer, then you know not to waste time trying to convince them of what they already believe. Conversely, if you discover that they are neutral on this matter when you suspected that they were already convinced, then you will obviously need to first convince them of second-hand smoke dangers before you can get them to join you in pushing for legal remedies to the problem.

The Semantic Differential

The semantic differential is a survey instrument that does not have the popularity of the Likert-scale. Nonetheless, it is particularly useful for ascertaining a statistical picture of an audience's perception of an idea, product, or person.

Semantic differentials work by word-association. They ask respondents to rate a "concept," be it an idea, product, or person, on a continuum that spans two bi-polar adjectives. For instance, suppose we wanted to know something about how our audience perceives Nuclear Disarmament.

We could design a set of semantic differential scales to help us "see" it as they "see" it. It might look like the following:

NUCLEAR DISARMAMENT

good _____ : _____ : _____ : _____ : _____ : _____ : _____ bad

safe _____ : _____ : _____ : _____ : _____ : _____ : _____ dangerous

undesirable _____ : _____ : _____ : _____ : _____ : _____ : _____ desirable

possible _____ : _____ : _____ : _____ : _____ : _____ : _____ impossible

illogical _____ : _____ : _____ : _____ : _____ : _____ : _____ logical

Our audience would be asked to respond to each scale by placing an X on the blank that would most closely reflect their views on nuclear disarmament. Then we would code the responses in a way similar to the way we would do it with Likert-scales. Here the blank closest to the positive adjective is assigned the number (1) and the blank second closest is assigned the number (2) and so on all the way up to number (7) which is assigned to the blank closest to the negative adjective. Again, the numbers for each respondent are added and divided by the number of respondents to get a "mean" for the audience.

With the set of scales we have proposed for our survey we might discover that our audience believes that nuclear disarmament is "good" and "desirable," but "impossible" and "dangerous." Therefore, our message must focus on convincing them that there are ways of achieving disarmament that are "possible" and "safe."

Likert scales and semantic differentials give the speaker a means of gathering indespensable psychographic data. If these instruments are used and analyzed with skill, then the speaker can design a persuasive message that is powerful by virtue of being on target.

In undertaking audience analysis you can rely on intuition or science, or both. Make sure that you give great thought to who your audience will be, what time of day you will speak, where you will speak, and what will occur just prior to your speech and what will follow it. All of these things make your audience what it is at that point in time. Too many speakers deliver a mediocre speech because they insist on delivering "the speech in the mirror" when they could deliver a much better speech by *adapting* to the immediate context. When appropriate, references ought to be made to earlier speakers and speeches, and even to events that will happen later in the day. In this way, the speaker demonstrates to the audience that he or she is aware of the reality that they all share.

When it comes to persuasive speaking, audience analysis requires that you be sales-oriented. Make a list of your assumptions. Why might the audience object to taking the action you want them to take? Identify these objections in your speech and show that they are not reasonable objections or that your suggested action will resolve them. The effective persuader identifies objections and overcomes them. Make the action that you want your audience to take both *possible* and *immediate*. They should find it relatively easy to start doing what you want them to do, and they should be able to start doing it right away.

One speaker wanted his audience to join a health club. By using a questionnaire he was able to identify three major objections that his audience had to joining. They were:

1. It's too expensive.
2. I don't know anybody there.
3. I'm embarrassed to go because I don't know how to use those machines.

In his speech he worked to overcome or minimize the significance of these objections. He made it possible, and immediately possible, for his audience to join a health club. First, he arranged for everyone in the class to receive a free, two-week membership to his health club. He handed out their membership cards with their names on them immediately after his speech. He overcame the other two objections by saying, "If you'll look on the back of that card, you will find my telephone number. Anytime you want to go to the club, you call me and I'll come pick you up. I'll introduce you around and show you how the machines work. I mean it, now. Call me." His speech resulted in four people (out of 25 in the class) buying permanent memberships. Good audience analysis made his success possible.

SUMMARY

Topic selection is a problem that haunts college students more than the professional because the professionals generally have speech topics given to them. College students must examine their backgrounds and present opinions and major areas of study to find topics that they care about. If this is achieved it will result in a more confident delivery and in a more credible message.

Audience analysis according to demographic and psychographic data is an essential process for the would-be persuader. The more a speaker knows about the audience, the greater are the chances of being truly persuasive. The audience dictates topic treatment, the style of argument, the nature of evidence, the style of delivery, the length of the speech, and even the speaker's mode of dress.

REFERENCES

Hart, R. (1977). *The political pulpit*. West Lafayette, Indiana: The Purdue University Press.
Jebb, R. (1909). *The rhetoric of aristotle: a translation*. Cambridge: University Press.
Lorch, F. *The trouble begins at eight*. Ames, Iowa: The Iowa University Press.
Williams, B. (1987). (Ed.). *Writer's market*. Cincinnati, Ohio: Writer's Digest Books.

Research
and Development

5

When planning to deliver a persuasive speech, or any speech for that matter, it is natural to try to begin by working on the introduction. It does not require much thought to realize what an illogical tendency this is. How can you write an introduction when you do know what you are going to introduce? It is like trying to develop the advertising for a product that does not exist. Just as business puts ideas into Research and Development before creating an advertising campaign, so should you research and develop your speech content before writing the introduction for that content.

In this chapter we will provide instructions and advice on how to research your persuasive speech topic. We will direct you to the sources that will be of greatest value and teach you how to "package" what you find so that your support material will add persuasive power to your arguments.

RESEARCH

Research—it is a nasty little word isn't it! Yet it doesn't have to center around dusty old books in a dimly-lit library. Research can be an exhilarating experience. Trust us, it really can be. Would your authors lie to you? We suggest that you quit thinking of it as research. Think of it as investigative reporting instead. If you were an investigative reporter, desperately seeking the most up-to-date information on a given subject, where would you go to get it? Where could you find information on the "cutting edge" of a modern problem? You would get it from the living experts, of course, because what is in print is already out of date.

Interviewing

Daniel Webster, perhaps the greatest lawyer of the 1800's, once said that if you want to be wise you should "converse, converse, converse with living [people], face to face, and mind to mind— that is one of the best sources of knowledge" (Whipple, 1897, p. xix). Universities are packed to the rafters with experts on every subject you can imagine, and on some you cannot imagine. Set up an interview with a professor or administrator or a member of the university staff who is an expert on your topic. Have your questions well planned so as not to waste their time. Even if you can only get five minutes for your interview, you will often come out with a quotable quote, an illustrative story, or a scientific study that will serve as support material for your speech. Additionally, these experts can often refer you to excellent articles on the subject and thus save you hours of "investigative" library work.

Sometimes these experts are so rarely approached that they are delighted to have someone interview them. In such cases you may find yourself trying to get rid of them instead of having them trying to get rid of you. This happened to one of our students who planned to persuade his audience not to steal campus toilet paper and towels for use in their apartments. True, an off-beat topic, but a serious one in terms of monetary costs to the university, as he found out. He sought out the man who was in charge of restroom supplies. The man had spent many years steaming over this problem and had kept elaborate records on the losses his department had sustained due to toilet paper and paper towel thieves. Our student said that he was practically barricaded in this staff member's warehouse office for over an hour as he proudly displayed his statistics and told his "war-stories" about trying to cope with the problem. From this information the student was able to deliver a much more credible and interesting speech than he would have presented otherwise, though we must admit that the speech was not particularly persuasive. We know this because most in the audience were laughing so hard that they kept sliding out of their chairs and into the aisles. Toilet paper theft, despite the very real costs to the university, is not easy to convey as a serious problem. Nonetheless, from this example you can still see the illustrative value of conducting personal interviews as part of your research effort.

Naturally, we suggest that you go beyond the university and into the community to conduct interviews as well. If your topic centers on the ethics of corporate takeovers then talk to a few stock brokers. If your topic concerns highway safety, interview some state troopers. One of our students did this for her research on seat-belt laws and heard some gruesomely persuasive stories and even picked-up a comment that is almost a motto among state troopers, and which became the closing line of her speech: "I never unbuckled a dead man." Persuasion, like comedy, has its one-liners. This is an example of a highly-persuasive one-liner, which would never have been part of our student's speech had she not bothered to do some interviewing. This means of conducting your investigation is generally more interesting, fruitful, and time-productive than most other investigative methods.

The Popular Media

Have you ever noticed that when you learn a new word it seems to pop up all over the place in the next few weeks? It seems as though, all of a sudden, everyone has learned the word and begun to use it. It has been used all along, of course, but you notice it more once you have had your attention called to it specifically. The same phenomenon is at work when you begin to investigate your speech topic. All of a sudden it will seem that the whole world is interested in your topic. In your everyday media exposure, watching television, listening to the radio, and reading your favorite magazines and newspapers, you will see and hear interviews with experts on your subject and read articles about them and by them in magazines and newspapers. Take advantage of this fortunate phenomenon by keeping pen and paper handy at all times. By so doing you will be ready to jot down any information or argument that may be of value in developing your speech content. Make sure that you also record where you read or heard it so that you can provide the source of the information. The citation of the source does not have to be incredibly specific, either.

For instance, there is no need to say, "On the February 18th, 1987, edition of '60 Minutes,' during an interview conducted by Diane Sawyer, Admiral Rickover said ———" Instead, put it in people language and say, "I was recently watching Diane Sawyer interview Admiral Rickover on '60 Minutes.' I was struck by something he said, something of great importance to everyone here today."

Sometimes you will hear something that is just ideal for your speech but you are unable to write it down verbatim. Does this preclude your using it? No. You can use it, as long as you let your audience know that it is not an exact quotation. This can be done with class, too. You can say, "I heard Paul Harvey give some advice on this matter the other day. He said something to the effect that ———" By using the phrase "something to the effect," your audience knows that it is not an exact quotation. It is not as desirable as the real thing, but there are times when the *idea* is more important to your point than the exact wording of the idea.

Retail Book Stores

Retail book stores are good sources for contemporary works on any subject. In the weeks prior to your speech, drop by your campus book store or by B. Dalton's or Walden Books in the mall and browse. You never know, you might find a book that is hot off the press and beautifully suited for your topic. Though you may not be able to afford the book, you can at least scan the contents and write down the title and author, as well as a good quotation or two. We doubt that most retailers would be pleased with our money-saving suggestion, so just remember, you didn't hear it from us, okay?

Check the magazine racks, too. There may be a solid and insightful article on your topic. You won't have to write anything down either, since you can probably afford magazines. In this way you can cite information that has been published in the same month as your speech. In some cases, because of magazine publishing tradition, you can even be "ahead of your time" by citing the November '87 issue when you deliver your speech in October '87! You don't need us to tell you that this practice will impress your audience and add to your credibility.

Corporate and Agency Sources

As a public relations service many corporations and public and private agencies distribute, free of charge, pamphlets and booklets on issues of importance to them. These are generally fine sources of support material for persuasive speeches.

Planned Parenthood has many pamphlets on the value of sex education. The American Rifle Association can supply you with endless data attesting to the need to resist anti-handgun legislation. Your local health club has many handouts on the life-long benefits of cardio-vascular exercise. The American Civil Liberties Union can give you more help on defending the First Amendment than you could ever use. MADD can certainly mail you massive support for punishing drunk drivers to the full extent of the law. For some information, however, you have to wait up to six weeks for a limited staff to mail you the pamphlet you want. Thus, you should not make delivery of your speech dependent upon receiving that particular pamphlet. Instead, you should plan on not getting it, and if it comes in time, then so much the better.

The Library Investigation

You knew we would get around to the library didn't you? Libraries are only overwhelming because of the overwhelming amount of information they house. As you would do with any other large task, if you will break it down into smaller tasks, then your library investigation will be less formidable. So get your notecards ready and let's go to the library. We will walk you through the necessary steps. For those of you who already know about library research, you have our permission to skip the tour. We will meet you at PERSUASIVE SUPPORT. See you there.

The Card Catalog

This is a reasonable place to begin, although it is not the best source for the most current information on most subjects. The card catalog will direct you to books on your subject, most of which will provide you with an historical perspective on the problem. You do not have to read entire books to get what you want. Use the table of contents and the index to help you focus on that part of the book that is most useful to you. Write the pertinent information on a note card, record the title, author, and copyright date, and move on. Don't allow yourself to be distracted. Remember your specific purpose and use your time to focus on that information that will help you achieve your persuasive goal.

The Reader's Guide to Periodical Literature

This is probably the most used source for speech preparation. It contains hundreds of thousands of references to articles published in popular magazines, all conveniently listed and cross-listed under appropriate subject headings. If you want to read about Col. Oliver North's involvement in "Irangate," then you can find articles listed under "Irangate" or "North." The listings provide you with the title of the article, the name of the publication, the date of the issue, as well as the page numbers for locating the article. From there, you simply go to the place in the libarary where that magazine is kept and read the article, writing down or photocopying the parts that are of interest to you.

Government Documents

Our federal government keeps more records than any other government in history. Consequently, the government documents section of the library is bursting with information just waiting for someone to use it. Do you want to know how much the Air Force spent on new jets in 1986? Government documents can tell you. Would you like to know how your congressman voted on farm subsidies last year? Government documents can tell you that, too. If you attend a public university, government documents can even tell you how much your professor makes. Yes, it does sound like a marvelous source for all kinds of trivia, but a bit of trivia becomes highly significant when it is the ideal fact to support one of your arguments. Ask for help in using government documents. You will probably need it.

Computer Searches

Though sophisticated computer searches are beyond the budgets of most college students, and relatively non-productive for persuasive speech preparation we might add, we do want to call your attention to in-house computer searches. The holdings of some libraries are completely accessible through computer terminals. Fifteen minutes on a terminal can save you hours on the stairs and in the stacks. Generally, all you have to do is to enter a key word for your subject area and the works concerning your subject will appear magically on the screen. Read the titles. If you want further information on a given book, the computer will give you instructions on how to call up an abstract. From the abstract you can decide whether you want to actually tramp around looking for the book or not.

Another type of in-house computer search concerns a catalog of periodicals. This is a computerized version of *The Reader's Guide,* though it usually will not give you access to as many sources as *The Reader's Guide.* Again, it works by locating all the articles related to the key word that you enter. Be prepared to pay a nominal fee for a print-out of the sources. It is an inexpensive service and worth every nickel you've saved for the xerox machines.

Newspapers

The newspaper room is such a wonderful place. Here in one large room are recent newspapers from across the nation and around the world. Obviously, if your topic is in any way related to current social trends or political developments, this is the room for you. A couple of hours here, if well spent, can give you more usable information than a whole stack of books. (Do not wear white.)

References for Quotations and Great Stories

Some speakers always seem to have just the right quote or story when they need it. The inexperienced audience member is overly impressed by speakers who adorn their speeches with lines from Shakespeare and tales of how the pyramids were built. Their breadth and depth of knowledge is so impressive as they wander throughout history and across literature to illustrate their arguments. There are people who can do this because they are truly brilliant, but most of us intellectual mortals need help, which is why we need reference manuals such as *Bartlett's Quotations.* This book, and similar ones, are in every library and invaluable to the would-be sophisticate. You use them by looking up a subject like "War" and there you will find three pages of great comments on war, from the Bible and literature and history. Select the one that best says what you wish to say and use it in your speech, making sure to cite the source of the quote. Don't be like the little kid with the hammer, however, the one who was so fascinated by the tool that he used it all the time and on everything, appropriate or not. In other words, don't cite Shakespeare just to sound cool. Make sure that you select the line because it really says what you want it to say, that it moves you in some way. Then, chances are good that your audience will be moved by it, too.

There are similar types of reference books that compile great stories, both humorous and dramatic. Persuasive speakers generally want dramatic stories more than they want a humorous ones. These manuals, too, are easy to use. If you want stories about great scientists, then look up "Science" or "Discovery" or "Invention" and you may well find a dramatic recounting of a golden moment in science that is just the perfect example to support your argument.

Vital Speeches of the Day

While working on your speech you may remember that the President said something about your subject that would be strong support for your position. *Vital Speeches of the Day* is the resource you need. For years it has printed the more significant and interesting speeches delivered in the United States, and sometimes other parts of the world. Representative speeches range from the President's "State of the Union Address," to a banquet speech by the Chairman of Texaco, to last years commencement address at Cooper High School in Abilene, Texas. To make *Vital Speeches,* a speech must be either important or inspiring. Therefore, it is understandably an exceptionally fine source of support material.

Librarians

Don't forget the people who make libraries possible. They are highly trained professionals in library science and know how to find just about anything your heart desires. What is even more wonderful is that they *love* to do it! If they didn't truly enjoy the challenge, they wouldn't be in the business. So when and if you get stuck, ask a librarian to rescue you.

Another benefit to securing the help of a librarian is that they have been helping speech students for years. They may have even helped someone who researched your topic and therefore know just the right sources to seek out. If you get lucky in finding a librarian who helped a student research your topic last term, we say wonderful, but don't forget to check sources that will make your speech an update of the one prior to yours.

We have referred you to all of the above sources so that you can locate interesting and persuasive support for your speeches. Please keep in mind that support material should only *support your* speech, it should not *become* your speech. Your personality should rise above your support, not get lost in it. A good rule of thumb is to make sure that at least three-fourths of your speech is comprised of your own words. Support material such as examples, direct quotations, and stories can make up the other fourth of your speech. By maintaining this ratio you should insure that your supports are serving only as aids to the speech and not crowding you out altogether.

PERSUASIVE SUPPORT

We have informed you of sources to which you can go to find persuasive support materials. We now wish to consider several types of support, to tell you specifically what you are looking for when you conduct your research.

Persuasive arguments consist of claims and support for claims. Every day of your life you will hear people make assertions about the world around you. They will say, "The Chicago Bears are the best team in the NFL" or "Harvard has the best business school in the country" or "Bill Cosby is the most successful comedian of this decade." You might respond, quite naturally, to any one of these claims by saying, "What makes you think that?" You are asking for "support" or "proof" for their claim. They, in turn, could respond to your question by saying, "Well, everybody knows that!" This is a blatant case of assertion without proof, or a claim without support. Such an argument is, of course, extremely weak. If the Chicago Bears claim were supported, however, by the evidence that they had won more games by a greater margin than any other NFL team this year, then the argument would be substantially strengthened. It would provide a basis for us to see why the person is thinking as he is. If we were to accept his criteria as a good measure of "best teams," then we might well be convinced by his argument.

We want to help you avoid the "assertion without proof" problem by helping you learn how to support your claims with the strongest evidence available. We will elaborate on several support strategies, including statistics (and how to use them), analogies, examples, and testimony. Visual support, which is rightfully a powerful form of support, requires a more lengthy treatment and has an entire chapter devoted to it later in this text.

Statistics

Every age has its primary form of evidence. One hundred years ago it is likely that expert and eye-witness testimony was the most prevalent evidence in use. Although they are still widely used, statistics are relied on even more now. Despite Disraeli's warning that there are "three kinds of lies: lies, damned lies, and statistics," statistics remain our primary form of evidence, and statistics show that this trend shows no signs of weakening. With every claim a person makes, it seems, someone says, "Let me see the data on that."

Perhaps statistics are so widely relied upon because they are our fastest means of getting information. When you go to buy a car, you ask for the numbers: "How many miles per gallon does it get?" "How fast does it accelerate from 0–60?" "What are the monthly payments?" The numbers that answer your questions play a persuasive role in your decision to buy or not to buy the car. When you search for a house to buy you ask similar questions: "How many square feet is it?" "How big is the lot?" "What are the property taxes?" "What is the total cost?" "What interest rates are aviailable?" "At what rate will the property likely appreciate?" Again, the answers to these questions will help determine whether you will purchase that particular home or not. Though it is indelicate of us to point it out, it is nonetheless true that even when someone is trying to convince you to accept a blind date with their cousin, you ask for the numbers.

We live in a society obsessed with numbers. At sporting events across the country fans scream "We're Number One!" Many olympic events are judged on a scale of one to ten, as is the physical attractiveness of those around us. Dow Jones analysts watch the leading economic indicators in order to predict whether the market will continue its bullish ways or slip into a bearish trend. Surveys on the president's "performance approval rating" are released almost every week. Television shows live and die by the Nielson ratings, as do records that either make or fail to make *Billboard's* "Top 40." Books can get a tremendous boost by making the *New York Times* Best-Seller list. And what about you? You are affected by that ever-haunting GPA because you know that when you graduate the numbers will, unfortunately, speak louder than most words.

Statistical Illustrations

There is a notion among many speakers that all they must do with statistics is to let the "numbers speak for themselves." This is not a good strategy, as numbers have never been terribly articulate entities. The speaker should help the audience see how the numbers support the argument being made. It is perfectly fine to assert that the "numbers speak for themselves" as long as you go right ahead and speak for them anyway. It is better to risk talking down to your audience just slightly than it is to leave them in a fog.

Many of the numbers we must cope with in this society have no real persuasive power because they are incomprehensible. A politician who shouts that we now have "a trillion dollar national deficit" and expects the American people to be outraged is ignorant of the ignorance most of us have about numbers greater than a million. Traditional wisdom would tell this legislator to break a trillion down into smaller units to make it more understandable. It could be expressed as "a thousand billion," which really wouldn't help very much because we are still left with a number that is incomprehensible. A visual analogy could be used by saying, "A trillion dollars, if laid end-to-end, would stretch to the moon and back three times." Though this is more helpful, we are still overwhelmed by the quantity, and underwhelmed by the its economic meaning. For incomprehensible numbers to be made comprehensible, and persuasive, they must be expressed in *human terms*. How do we best understand money? We understand it according to what it will buy and how long it will last. With this in mind, we might explain a trillion by first explaining a million and a billion in human terms:

> If you wanted a million dollars and I had it to give to you, I could give you a thousand dollars every day for three years. Think of it. Every day you could blow a thousand bucks! What fun! If you wanted a billion dollars and I had it to give to you, I could give you a thousand dollars every day, not for just three years, but for three *thousand* years. Now, if you wanted me to dole out a trillion dollars at the same rate, you would have to live to be as old as a dinosaur because it would take 3,000,000 years to do it. However, if you wanted your trillion dollars given to you on our original, three year plan, then your allowance would be about a billion dollars a day. You could never sleep late. You would have to get up early and get out there and spend your allowance. Every day would be a party, just the kind of party the federal government is having every day at your expense.

This kind of statistical illustration would serve our politician's goals much better, don't you think? It expresses the deficit in human terms. Another way to go about illustrating the same figure is to do as Walter Mondale did in the 1984 presidential race. He saw that there was tremendous apathy about the national defecit because no one seemed to understand exactly how serious the problem was. Some people had even suggested that we have a "Deficit Telethon" whereby Americans would be be asked to donate money to pull ourselves out of debt, which would have meant that every man, woman, and child in the country would have had to cough up over $8000.00. To illustrate this point in the most persuasive way possible, Mondale combined the enormous deficit, (an incomprehensible element), with two comprehensible elements (the tax man, and a newborn baby). The resulting advertisement showed the tax man presenting the screaming baby with an $8,000.00 bill for taxes owed upon birth. In so doing Mondale was able to personify (express in human terms) the tremendous burden the deficit is for all of us.

One final strategy for coping with large numbers like the deficit is not only to break down the number into smaller units, but to break down the size of the *problem* as well. This does not mean that you are attempting to minimize the severity of the problem; but quite the contrary, you are attempting to demonstrate the large-scale seriousness of the problem by proving its seriousness on a smaller, more meaningful scale. For instance, a speaker might say:

> As I speak our government is spending about $30,000 dollars each second. That wouldn't be so bad if it weren't for the fact that the U.S. treasury is only taking in about $22,000 each second. The difference of $8,000 the government borrows every second of every day to pay its bills. In fact, in the ten minutes that I've been talking so far, we Americans have plunged $4,800,000 deeper into debt. If you and I were to run our personal finances like this, we would soon be in deep trouble. The federal government is no different. It cannot escape economic law. (Adapted from "Numbers that Talk," 1984, p. 4.)

The federal deficit is one of the largest numbers we have to cope with today, but there are larger ones. What do you suppose is the largest statistic of all? It would have to be that number which never stops growing, the number that statisticians call "infinity." Strangely enough, it is not the scientists but the clergy that must communicate the meaning of infinity most often. They usually call it "eternity" and they have found some imaginative ways of communicating the concept. One of the more shocking statistical illustrations for eternity is still being used in a few pulpits today, though its origins can be traced back to the "hell-fire and brimstone" sermons of the 19th century. In those days, the apparent need of the most strict ministers was to scare their followers into "being good" by making them understand how long they would be in hell if they did not live highly moral lives. Some of these ministers said something akin to this:

> Suppose that once in a billion years a bird should come from some far distant planet, and carry off in its little bill a grain of sand, a time would come when the last atom composing this earth would be carried away; and when this last atom was taken, it would only be sun-up in hell. (Larson, 1962, p. 19)

We cite this example to show that even the largest of numbers can be expressed in very human, and in frighteningly impactful ways.

As science has probed further and further into the universe, it has also probed further and further into micro-universes. So not only are persuaders in need of statistical illustrations that make large numbers small, they are also in need of illustrations that make small numbers large. Only in this way can the scientists studying incomprehensibly tiny phenomenon persuade those who would fund their research that the work is important. John Schwarz uses a statistical analogy to explain the size of the "Planck length," the basic element in the work of Superstring theorists:

> In 1974 the late French physicist Joel Scherk and I proposed that elementary particles are not points but rather are one-dimensional curves called strings. These strings have zero thickness. Their lengths vary depending on the circumstances, but their typical value is the Planck length, 10^{33} centimeters. That's exceedingly small: the Planck length is as much smaller than an atom as an atom is smaller than the universe (Schwarz, 1985, p. 62).

We don't know about you, but we would rather fund the study of something that is "as much smaller than an atom as an atom is smaller than the universe" instead of that which concerns some mystical "Planck length." Just the ability to illustrate the number is persuasive as it demonstrates that the resarchers are studying what are probably the basic components of the universe.

Using statistical illustrations to make incomprehensible numbers understandable is the mark of a good communicator. However, the good *persuader* is not only one who can communicate the numbers, but one who can express their meaning in the most human of terms. Numbers only *stand for* realities. The persuader must work hard to translate the numbers into realities that the audience can see and feel.

Some of the people most successful at doing this are insurance agents. It is difficult to get potential clients to shell out $200 dollars a year for life insurance, so the agents will often say that the policy "costs only 50 cents a day." And they will go on to minimize the sacrifice by saying that all the client has to do is give up one soft-drink, or one cup of coffee each day, something that will be good for the client's health, as well as contributing to his family's future financial security.

There are those who employ the exact opposite strategy to make small numbers overwhelming. A speaker trying to get a group to quit smoking will say, "If you buy a pack of cigarettes every day you probably don't even feel that measly little dollar and twenty cents slip out of your hand. But if you had to buy a year's supply all at once you would find it a painful experience because you'd have to hand over $438.00! That's food for a month! That's two car payments!"

These strategic methods of communicating numbers persuasively are in use everywhere because of their effectiveness. It is entertaining to watch government debates over the funding of long-term projects. As the proponents are breaking the numbers down on one side of the room, their adversaries are adding them back up on the other side. The winner is often determined by the side that communicates its numbers in the most human terms.

Sometimes you will want to *question* the statistical interpretations of others as a means of supporting your argument. Observe how the following speaker does this.

> I detest the use of percentages only, and not actual numbers, so much so that I will give the audience a third example. Just 10 days ago a news item appeared in our local newspaper on the disease AIDS (acquired immune deficiency syndrome). The article was headed by "Study Shows 10 Percent of Blacks Only 4 Percent of Whites Have Aids." Most people will come quickly to the conclusion that 2.5 times more blacks than whites had the disease in the investigation; however, the use of actual numbers—which did not appear in the story—would show that 3 times more whites than blacks had AIDS in the study. (Alexander, 1987, p. 203)

Thus statistics may be used to directly support your argument or you may wish to refute or reinterpret "established" statistics in order to give your argument a fair hearing.

Surveys

If statistics are the primary form of evidence in this age, then the survey is one of the most prevalent methods used to gather statistics to prove our points. We Americans love surveys, particularly opinion surveys. We like to know what the majority of us think about all kinds of things, from the most significant to the most insignificant of issues. "80% of Americans Support Freeze on Nuclear Weapons" reads a headline in the *Washington Post*. "Drug abuse is the number one problem of our time, says 63% of Americans polled," reports Dan Rather on the *CBS Evening News*. *Entertainment Tonight* tells us that "62% of the *Moonlighting* fans who called the hotline want David and Maddie to get married." Advances in technology have made it possible for us to monitor ourselves to death. Yet we seem not to grow tired of it. We like to know what we collectively think and believe. In a democratic country, majority opionions have persuasive clout, since many people like to allign themselves with the majority. After all, is there not safety in numbers?

We can combine the power of numbers and the power of credibility by surveying only the most credible of samples. This is what makes the following persuasive:

> We asked a thousand doctors if stranded on a desert island which one medicine they would want along, Tylenol, Extra-Strength Tylenol, Advil, or Bayer? 44% chose Bayer. Bayer, the wonder drug that works wonders.

This is a strong argument because the sample is a large sample (1000), it is a credible sample (doctors), and the sample has to choose one product from a field of respectable products to be used in a specific situation. Nevermind that there is only one brand of aspirin in the set of choices, the advertiser lets you in on more than most of the medical-survey genre of ads let you in on. Just as easily they could have reported, "We asked doctors if they were stranded on a desert island what pain-reliever they would want to have along? 57% chose Bayer." This version is vague and ought to raise a few questions: How many doctors were surveyed, 10 or 100 or 1000? How many choices were they given, 2 or 10? Who did the surveying? If we really wanted to get picky we could ask a few more questions about both reports. How did they select the doctors to be surveyed? Were they randomly selected from across the country or were they all urban doctors living in Los Angeles? How many times was the survey conducted before the favorable 44% Bayer decision popped up? This last question is likely to be the most important question of all because conducting a survey over and over insures that, by pure chance, the desired results will eventually emerge.

Hopefully, this example will teach the kind of scrutiny you should take with you as you search for survey data to support your arguments. Ask yourself who did the surveying and do they have reason to be biased? Virtually all politicians who are behind shortly before an election have their own survey data to counter the data of the independent pollsters. Now who should we believe? For the same reason, consumer surveys that prove Ford cars have the highest "customer satisfaction ratings" of all domestic cars carry more weight when they come from *Consumer Reports* rather than Ford Motor Company. Seek out the unbiased sources of survey data. They have the persuasive power you want.

Incidentally, you can even conduct your own survey. If you are speaking on an issue such as "insufficient lighting on campus" you might stand out in a high pedestrian-traffic area and interview people. Interview 100 and report the results in your speech, admitting that it is not a scientific poll, but that it does show that a "good number of students feel that there should be more lights on campus."

When you use a survey in your speech, tell your audience who conducted the survey, and when possible, how they conducted it. How many people were involved? How were they chosen for the survey? When and where was it done? What were the results and what do those results mean in relation to your argument? This does not have to be a long and drawn-out, cumbersome task. It can be accomplished in a simple and elegant way.

It is well worth the effort to study ways that statistics are used to deceive so that you can learn to recognize fallacious conclusions when you see them. We suggest these books on the subject: *How to Lie with Statistics* by Darrell Huff and *The Art of Deception* by Nicholas Capaldi.

Analogies

Analogies may be the most powerful form of persuasive support available to would-be persuaders. Analogies work by asking the audience to see one thing in terms of something else. Just to make this definition clear we should consider the following slightly amusing analogy from *Rolling Stone,* which asks us to see watching soap operas in terms of drug addiction.

> Soaps are like recreational drugs—you rarely get involved on your own. Peer pressure accounts for a large percentage of recent converts. And, like dope, the first time has little effect. The second time you humour yourself into thinking you've experienced a bit of nirvana, and by the third viewing, you'll want to acquaint yourself with the local rehabilitation clinic, certain that you're in too deep (1984, p. 18).

This analogy begins by suggesting a general relationship between watching soap operas and taking recreational drugs, and then continues to draw out specific ways in which the two "unlike" things are "alike." This is why analogies are so powerful. They sometimes force audiences to see similarities in things that are, in reality, very different. For this reason analogies are the weakest form of support for formal arguments, and the strongest form of support for informal arguments. Let us explain this. Analogies persuade by claiming that if something is true in one situation it must be true in others as well. Since analogies are usually used to compare completely different phenomena, the end result is a weak "formal" link between the two things. For instance, a professor of neurology could try to help medical students get a grasp on the functions of the Central Nervous System by saying, "The Central Nervous System is the long distance service of the body. It has over 100,000 miles of wires and it sends messages over great distances in split seconds." This comparison is a strong form of support for an "informal" argument because the unitiated can be so easily convinced to see the Central Nervous System in terms of a telephone system. Later in their training, however, the medical students will see that the differences between telephone systems and nervous systems are far greater than the similarities. In the long run, those who would become research specialists in neurology would find the analogy technically misleading and confusing. Therefore, analogies are especially good tools for inspiring initial interest and fundamental understanding of theories, concepts, philosophies, and policies, but when pressed too far, analogies collapse for lack of formal, logical support.

As a consumer of persuasion it is good to recognize the weaknesses of analogies. As a producer, it is good to recognize their power because most of the time they help "unitiated" audiences understand complicated concepts in terms of the more simple concepts that they already understand.

O'Donnell and Kable have a wonderful way of describing the response of one who has been successfully persuaded. They say that such a person remarks internally, "I never thought of it that way before" or "I never saw it that way before" (1982, p. 9). Analogies are uniquely suited to help audiences "see" things in new ways. Consider how the following speaker helps his audience see their significance in a new light:

One Person—You—Can Make a Profound and Lasting Difference

It's easy to diminish our importance. The mathematicians tell us that in terms of size, our significance is infinitesimal. A map of the universe we know of would be 80 miles long. On that map, our galaxy would take up an 8½ × 11 sheet. Our solar system would be a molecule on that sheet. And Earth would be a speck on the molecule. The astronauts tell us that as they observe the Earth from outer space, they don't think about Star Wars defense systems. Instead they see Earth as one vulnerable ship Gallactica, riding through a cold and dangerous universe as the lone outpost of humanity.

We are the stewards of human progress on this planet. Human progress is a chain, and every generation forges a little piece of it. You've heard the old expression that a chain is only as strong as its weakest link. My challenge to you today is to do what you can to strengthen your link and thereby hand down a stronger chain to the next generation. (Sikorski, 1986, p. 615)

There are actually three analogies used in this excerpt. The first is a mathematical analogy to get us to see how insignificant we are in relation to the vastness of the universe. Yet through the second analogy we are taught our undeniable significance as the protectors of "the lone outpost of humanity." Because our species is so rare, we are therefore precious and important creatures. The third analogy uses the "weak link" theory to convince us that we all have a duty to perform in this mission to build a better and safer world. Thus the three analogies support beautifully Sikorski's original contention that one person "can make a profound and lasting difference." Now that you see how it works, go back and read it again just to appreciate the artistry of it.

If you still are not convinced of the power of analogies, keep in mind that Jesus Christ, a man who has been called "The Great Persuader," amassed a following of tens of thousands (millions over the centuries) with the flawless use of parables. And what are parables? They are nothing more than analogies in story form. Audiences love analogies and parables and stories because they are visual in nature and visual images lodge comfortably in the mind. Use analogies; you will find them to be effective forms of persuasive support because they help the audience see things as they haven't seen them before.

Examples

When students say, "I really like Professor Moore; she's a great teacher," we naturally want to know what Professor Moore does that makes her so respected. So we ask and invariably learn that she "makes things understandable by giving lots of good and clear examples for every idea she teaches." In short, she helps students grasp abstract ideas by providing concrete examples that illustrate them.

Speakers who use strong, illustrative examples give clarity to their ideas, and hence, persuasive power. We learn by example and we are persuaded by example. Throughout this book we have endeavored to provide you with the best examples of the concepts we think you should know, not only to make them clear, but to inspire you to use them, too. We have now come to that ironic point in the book where we must furnish you with examples of examples! Examples come in two forms, factual and hypothetical, and we will demonstrate (aren't you lucky) both of them.

Factual Examples

After you make a claim, "History teaches us that trade protectionism is a disastrous economic policy," or "All geniuses have one significant trait in common," or "Liberal Arts majors make the best management trainees," audiences want you to cite an example or examples to prove your point. Motivation speakers are loaded with factual examples from which they choose according to the occasion and the audience. Before Paul Harvey gives a public address, for instance, he leafs through an enormous notebook to find just the right true stories which will best support his claims for that particular audience. Motivation speakers prefer to use true, or allegedly true examples because audiences know that if having the right attitude honestly made a difference for famous and successful people, then the methods might work for them as well. Hope springs eternal!

We certainly wouldn't think of the satirist, Garry Trudeau, as a motivational speaker, but sometimes when he is not drawing his "Doonesbury" strip he ventures out onto college campuses to deliver commencement addresses, which are at least "attitude adjustment" speeches. In the excerpt which follows Trudeau attempts to convince the near-graduates of Wake Forest University of the rewards to be reaped from asking the "impertinent question." He employs a barrage of factual examples to illustrate and prove his claim.

> I first came across the impertinent question in the writings of the master inquisitor, Studs Terkel. He himself claims to have adopted it from the physicist Jacob Brownowski, who once told him, "Until you ask the impertinent question of nature, you do not get a pertinent answer. Great answers in nature are always hidden in the questions. When Einstein in 1905 questioned the assumption held for three hundred years that time is a given, he asked one of the great impertinent questions: 'Why? How do you know that my time is the same as yours?' "
>
> The impertinent question is the glory and the engine of human inquiry. Copernicus asked it and shook the foundations of Renassaince Europe. Darwin asked it and is repudiated to this day. Thomas Jefferson asked it and was so invigorated by it that he declared it an inalienable right.
>
> Daniel Defoe asked it and invented the novel. James Joyce asked it and reinvented the novel, which was promptly banned.
>
> Nietzsche asked it and inspired Picasso, who restated it and inspired a revolution of aesthetics.
>
> The Wright brothers asked it and their achievement was ignored for five years. Steven Jobs asked it and was ignored for five minutes, which was still long enough for him to make $200 million. (Trudeau, 1986, p. 620)

Examine that last line. Trudeau knows exactly who he is addressing. He took them on an historical jaunt, demonstrating constantly that fame and/or wealth awaited those who had the nerve and the genius to ask the impertinent question. Considering what we know about the modern college student, we would call that a most persuasive inducement to follow his advice.

If and when you find yourself in the fortunate position of having more factual examples than you can use, any of which would nicely support your argument, then use those that are closest to your audience in both time and space. If, for instance, you are trying to convince an audience that date-rape is a serious problem, cite examples of date-rape on your campus or on a nearby campus or within the state. You may use national examples to show that this is a problem everywhere, but until you bring it down to the local level, it does not "hit close to home." Naturally, if you can find cases of date-rape that have been reported within the last week, then this is more convincing evidence than reports from last year. To make a problem real, you must use examples which will convince your audience that the problem is near and of immediate concern.

Hypothetical Examples

When you cannot find the type of factual illustrations that you would like to have, or when your argument concerns some future occurrence, you may have to rely on hypothetical examples for evidence. That does not mean that you should create fantastic and unbelievable stories, but rather, illustrations that are valid based on the facts as you know them. Indeed if you say that "banning smoking in public will eventually lead to the banning of babies in public as well," your hypothetical case will seem so outlandish that your audience will conclude that you are "over-reacting," and therefore not sensible, and therefore not credible.

The heart and soul of the hypothetical argument is in the two words, "What if?" "What if this were to happen?" asks the speaker. Then the speaker goes on to answer his own question, gently taking his audience through the reasoning required to reach the conclusion that he wants them to reach. Kenneth Adelman, Director of the U.S. Arms Control and Disarmament Agency does this well in his speech, "Ballistic Missiles and SDI." He says:

> So let's imagine for a moment a world in which nuclear weapons were about to completely by eliminated. What kind of world would this be? What kinds of problems would we face? . . .
> Elimination of nuclear weapons would require the most extensive and intrusive system of on-site inspections anyone could imagine. It is hard to think of a major military or even industrial installation that could be legally exempted from inspection on demand. That would mean, in turn, unprecedented openness to foreign intrusion on the part of all nations. Thus far the Soviet Union has raised objections to even the most limited inspection arrangements. (Adelman, 1987, p. 181)

Through the hypothetical case Adelman is able to show how difficult it is to reach a safe and sane Arms-Control Agreement. He is also able to lay the blame for the impasse at the Russians' feet. Change only two words in this hypothetical example, Soviet Union to United States, and you would have an argument that would be equally effective for a Russian negotiator addressing a Soviet audience.

Besides creating the hypothetical situation, you have the option of creating the audience-centered, hypothetical situation, which means that you ask your audience to role-play in some way so that they will experience the thoughts and feelings of one in a given predicament. You can say:

> You are driving alone in a remote area of the Sonoran desert. Your car breaks down. There is no way to fix it and you are eighty miles from the nearest village. Chances that someone will happen by are nil. Your friends will not even know that you are overdue for two days. The 118 degree heat muddles your ability to think. You check your supplies and curse yourself for not having more foresight. Only a quart of water is left. You look up into the hopelessly blue sky and see turkey vultures circling high above. Do they know something you don't? You wonder if you should try to walk out of the desert or stay with your car. The choice you make will mean the difference between life and death. What will you do?

The audience-centered hypothetical example works best when it employs the indefinite "you" and present tense. You are asking your audience to think the thoughts and feel the feelings that you want them to experience right now. In this way you are putting them into the proper frame of mind for accepting the persuasive message that you wish to present.

Testimony

We will not belabor the point here. We assume that you understand the value of testimony as support for your arguments. Yet we include it to remind you to use it. Too many speakers say, "I don't need to quote anybody, I'm speaking on the oil industry and I'm an oil man myself." The consistently persuasive speaker will cite others, no matter what the subject and no matter what his expertise in the area. U.S. presidents frequently cite other U.S. presidents, sports stars quote each other, as do ministers and teachers and labor leaders and bankers and astronauts. The reason they do this is twofold: to show that they do not stand alone, and to borrow the words of someone who has said what they wish to say better than they can say it.

Here is a good, multiple use of testimony. Don't you think it bolsters the speaker's claim?

> Consider our universities. I think it's true to say that it would be very impossible for an active patriot [conservative], however high his or her academic qualifications, to be granted tenure by a majority of universities. I will quote briefly from a few people who address this subject. Thomas Sowell, a distinguished academic economist who has been a professor at UCLA and now a senior fellow at the Hoover Insititution at Stanford, said in his newspaper column of October 3, 1986: "The left does not have to think on campus, just chant and demonstrate and feel morally superior. They can win by intimidation on campus, given the favoritism of the faculty and the pliability of the administration."
>
> On June 17, 1986, Irving Kristol wrote in the *Wall Street Journal.* "Our universities as institutions, have moved rapidly and massively to the left—and more often than not, toward the extremities of the left." And about the same time Norman Podhertz summed up in the Washington Post: "It is hardly an exaggeration to say that the Ivy League colleges have become the most narrow-minded and bigoted communities since the passing of the old American small town."
>
> . . . Even that circumspect newspaper, *The Wall Street Journal,* editorialized on September 3 that "in the academic world today, the undoubted road to tenure begins with a full tank of genteel liberalism, a viewpoint often broad enough to accept intolerance of conservatives." (Roberts, 1987, p. 214)

Had Roberts just claimed that universities were becoming havens of the left-wing and thrown in only one testimonial to support his claim, we could have written him off as an alarmist. However, he cited four different people and sources, all credible, that agree with his general premise, which makes it difficult for us not to at least give his argument some credence.

SUMMARY

Prior to preparing any speech you should conduct a broad and thorough research effort in order to develop the content. Resource materials may be gathered by means of interviews, the popular media, retail book stores, corporations and agencies, and, library investigations.

During your investigative work you are searching for persuasive support materials which include statistics, analogies, examples, and testimony. If you use your support materials skillfully, you will add persuasive power to your arguments.

REFERENCES

Adelman, K. (1987) Ballistic missiles and sdi. *Vital Speeches of the Day.* LIII (6), pp. 181–182.

Alexander, B. (1987) Why be ugly when you can be beautiful? *Vital Speeches of the Day.* LIII (7) pp. 202–204.

Larson, O. (1962) *American infidel: Robert G. Ingersoll.* New York: Citadel Press.

Numbers that talk about people (1984, September). *Scholastic Update.* O'Donnell, V. & Kable J. (1982) *Persuasion: an interactive-dependency approach.* New York: Random House.

Roberts, P. (1987) The unilateral disarmament of the american spirit. *Vital Speeches of the Day.* LIII (7) 212–213.

Schwarz, J. (1985, November) The next step. *Science,* pp. 61–68.

Sikorski, G. (1986) Will and vision. *Vital Speeches of the Day.* LII (24) pp. 613–615.

Soaps can be addicting (1981, October). *Rolling Stone.*

Trudeau, G. (1987) The impertinent questions: star wars and skepticism. *Vital Speeches of the Day.* LII (24) pp. 619–621.

Whipple, P. (1897) *The great speeches and orations of Daniel Webster.* Boston: Little & Brown.

Organizing the Persuasive Message

6

In a public speaking text by Verderber (1979), one principle of speech cited is: "Effective speaking involves organizing material so that it develops and heightens the speech's specific purpose (p. 49)." On the other hand, an exploration of research on the persuasive effects of organization led O'Donnell and Kable (1982) to reach a conclusion that appears to contradict Verderber: "Organization—or the lack of it—does not 'make or break' the persuader. . . ." While the effects of organization are not always clearly discernible, it is believed that the presentation order should contribute to the receivers' interest and help the receiver process what is being said.

Some speeches are relatively free of organization. Such "rambling" patterns of emotional stimuli are usually part of a rally or demonstration (Jeffrey & Peterson, 1983). Nevertheless, a great deal of research indicates that humans have a strong need to *structure* their existence (Berne, 1964; Brooks, 1978; O'Donnell & Kable, 1982). Indeed, Berne (1969) refers to a structure hunger which all humans have. This structure hunger is what causes people to behave in ways that occupy time. We need some order just to maintain sanity. If we have such a need for order, then it follows that speakers should structure their messages in ways that make sense or in ways that people can at least make sense of. Quite simply we are saying that you should provide some order to your speeches just to meet the human need for order.

Funadamentally, any communicated message will contain an introduction, body, and conclusion. Conventional wisdom provides us with the old saw: "tell them what you're going to tell them, tell them, and then tell them what you've told them." The preceeding maxim on how to organize the parts of a speech is not always true. Adaptation of an idea which will not be well received requires that you avoid telling the audience "what you're going to tell them." For example, if you intend to persuade the faculty at your college that a pay raise could cause great problems with the state budget, and the pay raise should not be desired, you would want to broach the subject slowly. The key would be to successively progress toward the issue with small bits of common concern. One student gave such a speech about the issue of faculty pay raises in a state which currently has no state income tax:

> For the first time Texas has an alarmingly high crime rate. The economy is believed to be the cause. Plummeting oil prices and failing agricultural businesses have plunged this state into a great recession. Human services will be cut back. Some state institutions may close. Many employees will lose their jobs.
>
> With state revenue continuing to plummet, and with the governor's commitment to eliminate red ink, it is amazing we have seen no new taxes. Talk of a state income tax has been heard. In this climate, if state university profesors expect a salary increase they will have to fight a difficult and uphill battle. . . .

If the student had begun instead with an abruptly direct statement of what the speech was about, for example: "Today I'm going to tell you why faculty at state universities should not expect a pay raise," The faculty audience would have been much less receptive!

Apparently, you do need a certain amount of knowledge of your options and application of organization fundamentals if you are to arrange your persuasive message in a way which will maximize the impact. The focus in this chapter will be on organization of the entire message: introduction, body, and conclusion. The chapter on introductions and conclusions should not be overlooked, however, in order to make those parts most effective.

In beginning to organize a persuasive message, after examining your pupose and gathering material, you must decide what the main topics or main points are going to be. The MAIN POINTS may be thought of as the central features of your message. You should take care in choosing main points, be precise in how you word them, and order the points based upon your strategy for the speech (Lucas, 1983). Clearly, the order in your message must be a logical interrelation among the main points. That interrelationship may emerge out of the topic itself. For example, if you were wishing to convince your audience that the Reagan Administration violated the constitution in the 1986 Irangate scandal, you would probably choose to arrange events, and therefore main points, in a chronological sequence. A time pattern is but one way of ordering material.

PATTERNS OF ARRANGEMENT

We will examine some options in patterns of arrangement and application before turning to one highly recommended alternative to be emphasized. Traditionally, the choices for an organizational pattern include: (1) chronological order, (2) spatial sequence, (3) topical pattern, (4) causal arrangement, (5) problem-solution, (6) pro and con, (7) general to specific, and (8) specific to general.

Chronological Order

Chronological or time order is an arrangement based upon when events occurred. This sequence may be based on reverse time order (starting with most recent and progressing to least recent) or may begin with the oldest event and progress forward in time (Brooks, 1978). It is risky to assume that a dry rendition of "this happened and then this" will produce a stimulating speech. You must add to the chronology by developing and supporting the events in order to maintain interest. A time order would be used to trace the history of an event, to describe a process, or to relate personal experience (Jeffrey & Peterson, 1983).

Spatial Order

A spatial or geographic pattern of arrangement is not as likely to be used in a persuasive context. The main topics are arranged based upon where they are physically located. Messages which relay information would be a more likely vehicle for spatial arrangement, although one might use a spatial organization for a persuasive speech that concerns geographic issues, such as flood control, weather hazards, earthquake trouble spots, or economic differences between regions of the country. The key to effective use of this organizational pattern is to show spatial location relates topic areas to one another (Jeffrey & Peterson, 1983).

Topical Order

Topical patterns are used to arrange material according to categories of a subject. As an example, in assessing the "damage" done in the last four years by a given incumbent politician, one might divide the damage into the following topic areas: business, education, deficit spending, and crime. Each topic is considered to be a part of the whole area investigated in the message (Brooks, 1978). The topical arrangement is useful for logical consideration of a controversial subject, and it allows for extensive development of subtopics (Jeffrey & Peterson, 1983). However, some communicators choose this pattern (because of the logic of the topical approach) even when another might be more effective (Brooks, 1978).

Causal Order

Many speeches which advocate or persuade use a *causal* pattern, developing from known *cause to* reasoned *effect* or from known *effect* to projected *cause*. In analyzing the effects of an increasing interest in fundamentalist religion, one might postulate that the cause is the powerful use of mass media to "spread the word" (effect to cause). In developing a rationale opposing mandatory drug screening of adolescents without just cause, a speaker might analyze a law with mandatory sanctions and reason to the potential effects of lack of trust and/or invasion of privacy (cause to effect).

Problem-Solution Order

A common logical pattern which relates closely to causal arrangement is the problem-solution pattern. This pattern may well be adaptable to every persuasive speech which contains a rational element of argument (even though it may not always be the best choice). Problem-solution development demonstrates to the receiver an area in need of action, and poses the persuader's answer or best solution to the problem. This pattern forms the basis for the motivated sequence described later in this chapter.

Pro and Con Order

A pro and con pattern of arrangement examines those arguments for and against each sub-issue to be considered within a major topic area. The pro and con technique demonstrates a clear consideration of alternative views. Of course, you may well give more pros for your view and more cons for opposing views. However, one can achieve greater effectiveness from a presentation which creates the illusion of balance because therein is the implication of objectivity. The audience is treated as informed and mature, and you will have anticipated counterarguments (O'Donnell & Kuble, 1982).

General to Specific Order

The general to specific or deductive pattern of arrangment is utilized when an audience is receptive to the major ideas prior to the speech (Jeffrey & Peterson, 1983). A politician endorsing what some call the Reaganomics approach to solving the woes of our economy might begin with two major ideas on which most would agree: that we don't want higher taxes and we do want a balanced budget. Most taxpayers would agree in principle with the two generalizations. Given that general framework, the persuader would then examine specifically where it would be necessary to make cuts and "tighten the belt" in order to balance the budget.

Specific to General Order

A specific to general or inductive pattern might be used with a more hostile audience (Jeffrey & Peterson, 1983). In this pattern, several specific instances are drawn together to show a general principle. In endorsing a controversial generalization such as: students need to bear a greater percentage of the cost of higher education through tuition hikes, a speaker would probably find college students somewhat hostile. However, if the speaker began by developing specific points of agreement, the persuasive intent of raising tuition might succeed. The specific points might include: the quality of instruction as related to pay raises for teachers; the quality of support services such as library resources and library access and costs; the fact that only a tiny percentage of the cost of one's education is covered by tuition, and the crisis in the state economy. These specifics might provide support for the generality about the need for tuition hikes.

Of course, no pattern is foolproof. However, as we noted, the topic itself may suggest a pattern. Your attention to what you want to accomplish may provide you with a choice of pattern. Learning to outline can be an important enabling skill in organizing messages as well, but we will not discuss outlining in any detail.

It is probably best to focus on only one primary mode of arrangement. If, in organizing your message, you have difficulty in relating one pattern to another or in achieving a balance among key ideas, you may need to try another pattern. The range of main points is usually two to six, with three being the ideal (c.f. Jeffrey & Peterson, 1983, Verderber, 1979; Lucas, 1983).

TECHNIQUES FOR ORGANIZING

Once a pattern has been employed, the persuasive message sender should consider the use of a variety of techniques which aid the receiver in following the pattern of organization. The best known of these techniques include: transitions, internal summaries and previews, signposts, interjections, and mnenomics.

Transitions

Transitions are the semantic bridges between ideas. A transition might be a single word, a phrase or sentence, or a group of phrases or sentences. Generally, a transition refers to both the idea just completed and the idea about to be examined (Lucas, 1983). Transitions hold the speech together like glue (O'Donnell & Kuble, 1982), and transitions allow the speaker to examine the interrelationships between main ideas (Jeffrey & Peterson, 1983). Transitions may signal addition or amplification, contrast, example or sequence, conclusion, and time or place (Munter, 1982). Examples of transitions include the following:

- *In addition* to the arms for hostages issue, we must *also* deal with the Contra military aid.
- Having *completed* our examination of Iranian arms sales, let us *turn to* the issue of Contra aid.
- *Not only* are we dealing with Iranian arms sales, *but also* with channeling money to Nicaraguan rebels.
- We will deal *first* with Iranian arms deals and *subsequently* with Contra aid.

Other words used as transitions include: furthermore, besides, next, again, similarly, too, but, or, nor, still, yet, on the other hand, for instance, therefore, then, consequently, simultaneously, so far, and until now (Munter, 1982). Transitions bind ideas together for both speaker and audience. We cannot neglect this device in planning and organizing speeches.

Internal Summaries and Previews

Internal summaries and previews serve a function similar to that of transitions. The receivers' attention is focused on a critical idea and how it relates to the larger issue(s) of the speech. Both preview and summaries reinforce critically for the listener. If an idea is highly important, complex, abstract, or technical; a summary is helpful (Jeffrey & Peterson, 1983). A preview helps prepare the audience to listen to key ideas (Jeffrey & Peterson, 1983; Lucas, 1983). Sometimes, summary and preview can be used in tandem as a lengthy transition. An example is shown below.

> We have just examined four reasons for the Reagan Administration's invasion of Grenada. We will now examine the events which took place on the day of the assault which will give us an indication of the sophisticated planning that went into the exercise.

Signposts are a common technique for identifying main points. Usually the signpost is simply a letter or a number such as "first," "second," "third," or "A," "B," "C," etc. It is important to be consistent (if "one" is first then "b" is *not* second). It is also important in signposting to signpost *all* points of equal importance, rather than signposting the first and third out of five main points, for example. A simple example of signposting is shown below.

> On examining the humanness of the male of the species, three things are abundantly clear in male dealings with women:
>
> *First,* a man puts his needs ahead of the needs of his mate or significant other.
>
> *Second,* when a man communicates with a woman, his listening skills disappear.
>
> *And, third,* a man's sexual interests override any real appreciation of the total woman present.

Interjections

Interjections are a form of signpost which indicate a crucial idea. Interjections take such forms as "Now, this is key," and "Most important is . . . ," and "Critical to the thrust of this speech is this central theme: . . ." Interjections help focus or emphasize and provide something that oral discourse requires. In receiving written messages, the reader can go back and review to find key points in the message. However, speech communication is transitory, so the emphasis must be interjected (Jeffrey & Peterson, 1983).

Mnemonic Devices

Finally, a persuasive message may use mnemonic devices to join ideas together. An acronym may help the audience retain a series of points in a topical arrangement. A speech on coping with the problem of teenage preganancy might utilize the acronymn S.T.O.P., as follows:

Sensitivity to the other person's personal or internal conflicts.

Training in the biological aspects of intercourse.

Orientation toward real intimacy.

Prudence regarding the inhibition-lowering effects of alcohol and drugs.

Of course, any trick which reinforces memory will do. No doubt you know of many such devices already.

An awareness of an incorporation of the techniques described herein will enhance the receiver's capacity to follow the main ideas in your persuasive message, thus increasing the likelihood of success in accomplishing your purpose.

As a way of bringing about a synthesis of organizational structure, we would like to offer a pattern of organization which has been highly touted and widely used. Any method can be exploited more or less effectively, but his model, the Motivated Sequence has stood the test of time as well as any model.

THE MOTIVATED SEQUENCE

Earlier, in describing the problem-solution pattern of development, we claimed that any message which had a rational element could use this pattern. Since most messages include a logical component, we believe the motivated sequence is the most widely applicable pattern. This pattern was first developed by Alan H. Monroe, and Monroe and Ehninger (1969) and others have continued to promote the motivated sequence through at least nine editions of one of the most widely used texts in the field of speech communication.

In part, the motivated sequence owes its success to the psychology of John Dewey. The sequence is an application of systematic problem solving as formulated by Dewey. According to this model, the five steps for motivating an audience are:

1. ATTENTION
2. NEED
3. SATISFACTION
4. VISUALIZATION
5. ACTION

The first step, A T T E N T I O N, is to gain and maintain the receivers' attention. This is usually part of the introduction and takes such forms as the rhetorical question, the startling statement, the quotation, the anecdote, and the use of illustration. The goal is to engage something which will stimulate the audience's need to receive what you have to say. You should, in the attention step, try to find something in the receiver's frame of reference which will interest him/her. Try to establish common ground. From the perspective of your audience, give your "attention" step the "what's in it for me?" test of validity.

Once you have engaged the receivers' attention, you must describe a problem and how it relates to the receiver: you must show a N E E D. A fully developed need step: states concisely the problem, illustrates the problem, shows its seriousness, and points the problem at the receiver. All of the substeps in the development of need are not always present (Monroe & Ehniger, 1969), but pointing the need, showing how the problem affects the receivers is quintessential.

Following the clear establishment of a need, the persuader must demonstrate S A T I S - F A C T I O N of the need, or how to solve the problem presented. In the satisfaction step, the persuader's task may be: to state a solution, to explain it in detail, to show by theory and practice how the solution solves the problem, and to answer anticipated counterarguments (Monroe & Ehninger, 1969). The task might include any or all of the subtasks above, but the desired audience response is "this is a good and workable solution to the problem the persuader pointed at me."

Satisfaction of the need is reinforced by the project or V I S U A L I Z A T I O N step. In this step, the persuader visualizes either the benefits of the proposed satisfaction step (positive results) or the harms accrued (potential negative results) if the satisfaction step is not engaged. Occasionally, the persuader will discuss *both* the positive results and the potential negative results. In any case, the purpose is to intensify the receiver's desire for the proposed solution (Monroe & Ehninger, 1969).

The fifth and final step in the Motivated Sequence is a call for A C T I O N. A call for action or approval is needed in any speech to persuade. In a speech to actuate, you may want listeners to translate your posed need and satisfaction into something *done*. If the message is not intended to actuate but to convince, your action step may call for approval or declaration of agreement. The action step is usually a part of the conclusion, and takes the form of a final appeal or a focus upon the thrust of the speech.

The following is a skeletal framework of a speech to convince. The subject is instructional accountability in college teaching.

ATTENTION   You are being ignored! You have been ignored for years in favor of printed matter which is rarely read by more than a select few. What's worse, the quality of your education may well be suffering from a doctrine you may not have heard of, the publish or perish doctrine.

NEED   Basically, the way major universities assess the quality of their faculty is subjective and counterproductive. The most commonly cited reason for denial of tenure or non-renewal of a teacher's contract is lack of publication in scholarly journals. Despite the recent Carnegie Commission report on the decline in the quality of undergraduate education, quality of instruction is not considered. While number of publications and communication in the classroom may overlap, they do not always. The effect on us as college students is obvious: we are left out of the whole process. Even when you complete teaching evaluations, they are looked on by seven out of ten deans as reflective of the popularity of a teacher. Moreover, student evaluations of professors are widely used as an assessment by exception. In other words, only when the weight of a majority indicates a *problem* do college administrators take heed. In fact, the demonstrated value of exceedingly positive teaching evaluations has been shown to be negligible in retention and promotion decisions. *You have no impact on keeping quality instructors.*

SATISFACTION	The problem calls for a need to provide better feedback. We require objective evaluations which are objectively reported and figured as at least 51% of the formula for retention, tenure, and promotion. Students know when the instructor is ill prepared, incapable of communicating well, or focused upon something other than communication in the classroom. What's more, the student has been shown to be the most objective assessment in a recent issue of the *College Student Journal*.
VISUALIZATION	When we have more of a say in who our quality instructors are, we will enjoy the benefits of better undergraduate education, more stimulating classes, and mutual respect between those who educate and those who come to be educated.
ACTION	It is time for our voice to be heard. If we are not made an integral part of the process, we'll forever remain the ones left out of any plans for improving the quality of our own institutions of higher learning.

SUMMARY

There is a great deal of difference between the execution of organizational styles for informational and persuasive speeches. Whereas traditional wisdom would seem to say that "logical" order makes for the most persuasive speeches, controlled studies have not shown this to be the case. Audiences make sense of speakers in spite of their poor organization. Nonetheless, this is not to say that we should cast all order to the wind. Since we all have a need for order, speakers should provide some visible and tangible structure in their speeches.

The organizational styles include chronological, spatial, topical, causal, problem-solution, pro and con, general to specific, and specific to general orders. The speaker should attempt to use transitions, internal summaries and previews, signposts, interjections, and mnemonics as techniques that will help the receiver follow the organizational pattern.

Monroe's Motivated Sequence is an easy-to-follow and effective persuasive organizational style for speeches to convince and speeches to actuate. The motivated sequence consists of attention, need, satisfaction, visualization, and action.

REFERENCES

Berne, E. (1969) *Games people play: the basic handbook of transactional analysis*. New York: Ballantine Books.

Brooks, W. D. (1979) *Speech communication* (3rd ed.) Dubuque, Ia: Wm. C. Brown Company.

Jeffrey, R. C. & Peterson, O. (1983) *Speech: A basic text* (2nd ed.) New York: Harper & Row Publishers.

Lucas, S. E. (1983) *The art of public speaking*, New York: Random House, Inc.

Monroe, A. M. & Ehninger, D. (1969) *Principles of speech communication* (6th ed.) Glenview, IL: Scott, Foresman, and Company.

Munter, M. (1982) *Guide to managerial communication* (2nd ed). Englewood Cliffs, N.J.: Prentice-Hall, Inc.

O'Donnell, V. & Kable, J. (1982) *Persuasion: an interactive-dependency approach.* New York: Random House, Inc.

Verderber, R. (1979). *The challenge of effective speaking* (4th ed) Belmont, Cal.: Wadsworth Publishing Company, Inc.

Walter, O. M. (1982) *Speaking to inform and persuade* (2nd ed.) New York: MacMillan Publishing Company, Inc.

Persuasive Introductions and Conclusions

7

The beginnings and endings of persuasive messages receive a great deal of attention in textbooks. Brooks (1978) cited three studies from the 1930's and 1940's on speech introductions and conclusions. Our first reaction to such studies is that there must have been some really bored people teaching speech communication half a century ago. On the other hand, the studies do offer some data for consideration.

The three studies cited by Brooks indicate that:

1. Introductions constitute eight to nine percent of a speech.
2. Conclusions constitute 5.1 to 9.0 percent of a speech.
3. The eleven kinds of introductions most frequently used are: reference to subject, audience, occasion, current events, or something personal; quotation; anecdote; startling statement; question; humor; and historical reference.
4. The most frequently used conclusions are: challenge, quotation, summary, vision of the future, appeal, inspirational advice, proposal of the solution, question, and reference to the audience.

As a child of four can plainly see, there are numerous ways to begin and end a speech. If one turns to other texts, one will see different lists of techniques. Why bother to look at lists? We have no idea. After all, many introductions include more than one technique (as do many conclusions). What we shall do in this chapter, therefore, is to examine the purposes for each of these two parts of a speech and look at beginning and ending strategies through a few examples.

INTRODUCTIONS

As we stressed in the chapter on Research and Development, the body of the speech should be developed first. Once that is done, you may begin working on the introduction for the content. The introduction "sells" the body. It is the means by which audiences are seduced into the central content. If you fail to "grab" the audience here, you will probably fail in your persuasive purpose, too.

As a persuasive communicator, you may find the subgoals of introductions useful and enlightening. Lucas (1983) identified four subgoals: getting attention and interest, revealing the topic, establishing credibility and goodwill, and previewing the body of the speech. Jeffrey and

Peterson (1983) indicated three purposes for the introduction: arousing interest, creating a favorable impression for the speaker and topic, and preparing the audience to listen intelligently. Either set of purposes would serve the creator of a persuasive introduction. We will offer our own checklist against which you may wish to measure your introduction.

An introduction should accomplish one or more of the following:

1. Seize the attention of the audience and hold it.
2. Establish the credibility of the speaker.
3. Prepare the audience to listen.

The desired qualities of brevity and directness in introductions are difficult to achieve. Many speakers include all manner of unnecessary information in their introductions. For instance, one speaker began this way: "I am here today to talk about the need for reducing the numbers of whales killed in the Northern Pacific. Last year over 8,000 whales were harpooned and slaughtered by greedy fishermen." To say "I am here today" is superfluous. It is like beginning a letter by writing, "I am writing you a letter . . ." Just as the recipient of the letter doesn't need such ridiculous information, neither does the audience need to know that the speaker "is here today." Note that if the speaker were to drop the first sentence of the introduction entirely, the second sentence would make a more effective start: "Last year over 8,000 whales were harpooned and slaughtered by greedy fishermen." We have found this advice to be incredibly consistent in its wisdom. Once your introduction is composed, ask yourself if your first sentence is necessary and if the second sentence wouldn't be a better place to begin.

Additionally, avoid saying things such as "I hope everyone can hear me out there" and "you'll have to excuse my voice—I have a really bad cold" and "My name is Laura and I'm a junior and I'm happy to be here. . . ." All of these things are the equivalent of testing a microphone by saying "testing ONE—TWO—THREE," only in this case you're testing your voice to see if it's actually going to work. Poised speakers launch right into a significant sentence and adjust their volume by reading the faces of those in the back of the audience. The temptation to apologize for a "cold" is understandable, but like speech anxiety itself, the weak and scratchy voice is ten times more noticeable to the speaker than it is to the audience. The first thing out of your mouth is critical, so be sure that it begins immediately to move your audience toward the acceptance of your persuasive goal.

We will now turn to a consideration of several introduction strategies for persuasive messages. We will cover the occasion-based introduction, the humorous introduction, as well as the use of hypothetical situations, rhetorical questions, startling statements, quotations, and stories.

Occasion-Based Introductions

If the occasion and audience merit it, you might begin by referring to those present and/or to your purpose for being there. Garry Trudeau does this in his address to the graduates at Wake Forest University. He says:

> Ladies and Gentlemen of Wake Forest: My wife, who works in television, told me recently that a typical interview on her show used to run 10 minutes. It now runs only five minutes, which is still triple the length of the average television news story. The average pop recording these days lasts around three minutes, or, about the amount of time it takes to read a story in *People* magazine. The stories in *USA Today* take so little time to read that they're known in the business as "News McNuggets."

Now, the average comic strip only takes about 10 seconds to digest, but if you read every strip published in the *Washington Post,* as the President of the United States claims to, it takes roughly eight minutes a day, which means, a quick computation reveals, that the Leader of the Free World has spent a total of 11 days, 3 hours and 40 minutes of his presidency reading the comics. This fact, along with nuclear meltdown, are easily two of the most frightening thoughts of our time.

There's one exception to this relentless compression of time in modern life. That's right— the graduation speech. When it comes to graduation speeches, it is generally conceded that time— a generous dollop of time—is of the essence.

This is because the chief function of the graduation speaker has always been to prevent graduating seniors from being released into the world before they've been properly sedated. Like all anesthetics, graduation speeches take time to kick in. So, I'm going to ask you to bear with me for about a quarter of an hour. It will go faster if you will think of it as the equivalent of four videos. (Trudeau, 1987)

In this introduction Trudeau identifies with the graduates. He lets them know that he understands their need to "get on with it," but that tradition forces him to consume some time in his address. By focusing on both the occasion and the purpose of the speech, he prepares the audience for the more serious message that will follow.

The Humorous Introduction

It is possible to make use of self-deprecating humor to simultaneously entertain and build credibility for yourself. After all, we like people who are big enough to poke fun at themselves, people who, no matter what they have accomplished in life, are not overly impressed with their achievements. Governor Mario Cuomo of New York uses this strategy in introducing his commencement speech to the graduates at Harvard:

It's an honor to share this day with you. And since this is Harvard and your motto is 'Veritus'—truth—let me be completely truthful with you. I know I wasn't your first choice as a speaker here today. Nor your second. Nor your third.

You invited three of America's funniest men . . . then when Larry and Curley and Moe all declined, you invited me. (Cuomo, 1985, p. 581)

Here is another example of a speaker using self-deprecating humor to build his credibility. The speaker is a political economist and aims the humor at his profession:

Thank you very much for that introduction. I very much appreciate that you did not introduce me as an economist. A fellow once told me that if you took all the economists in the world and laid them end to end, they'd never reach a conclusion. Another fellow told me if you took all the economists in the world and laid them end to end, it would be a damn good thing. (Roberts, 1987, p. 212)

The Hypothetical Situation

A hypothetical situation is particularly useful for getting an audience focused on the central topic of the speech. The following hypothetical, role-playing introduction accomplishes this nicely. It forces the audience to think the thoughts and feel the feelings that one in this situation would really experience.

Your father had Huntington's disease. So did your grandfather. Before the age of fifty, each suffered the debilitating and slowly degenerating effects of this disease. Your family suffered, too, seeing the complete destruction of the personalities they had known and loved. Every member of the family has agonized over the possibility that this genetic time-bomb ticks inside of them. Now you have discovered a test which will indicate with absolute certainty whether you will suffer the fate of your father and grandfather. If the test is positive, you will definitely get the disease. If it is negative, you will be free of worry. Will you take the test?

The question at the end of this example is indicative of a common attention device. Often a question will "bring an audience into" your thinking. Sometimes you may wish to *begin* with a question, a rhetorical question.

The Rhetorical Question

Most of the time rhetorical questions are defined as questions to which the speaker does not expect an answer. More importantly, a rhetorical question *cannot be answered,* at least not in a short period of time. "How many of you are sophomores?" is *not* a rhetorical question. It takes no thought to answer the question. Think of rhetorical questions as *persuasive questions.* They should get the audience thinking in the direction of your topic.

WHAT WILL THIS COUNTRY BE LIKE WHEN 10,000,000 PEOPLE HAVE AIDS?

This is a rhetorical question because there can be no immediate answer. When you ask a rhetorical question, make sure that you *pause* for a few seconds afterward. Allow the enormity of the question to sink in. Perhaps ask it twice. Then, the rest of your introduction can be a set of follow-up questions that probe further the problem originally posed. For instance:

What will this country be like when 10,000,000 people have AIDS? Who will care for all of these people? Will there be enough hospital beds to go around? How will we cover the enormous health costs of providing these unfortunate souls with the care they deserve? Or is all of this thinking just the product of mass hysteria and not something that will ever happen anyway?

Questions are popular ways of beginning speeches. They interest audiences by implying that the speaker will provide some answers in the speech to the provocative questions raised in the introduction.

The Startling Statement

Outrageous remarks and surprising statistics and booming voices all make for startling introductions. A speaker who walks quietly to the podium and screams "RAPE!" at the top of her lungs will certainly get attention. At this point she can proceed in a classy manner or in a non-classy manner. If she were to say "now that I have your attention I'd like to talk to you about rape," we would say that her technique is showing and call her introduction a "cheap trick." However, if she were to follow her scream by saying, "How would you feel if you screamed that over and over and no one ever came to help? How would you feel if you screamed with all your might and became convinced that you and the rapist were the only ones hearing it?" This follow-up is much better because it provides a *reason* for the scream. It shows that it was "called for."

Still, there are more sophisticated ways of using the startling statement. Examine these:

Before this speech is over, somewhere in the United States, a woman will be raped.

In the next five minutes, in the United States alone, over a hundred homes will burst into flames. When those fires have been extinguished, two people will have died, 47 will have been maimed, scarred, or disfigured for life, and a quarter of a million dollars will have gone up in smoke.

THREE MILLION gallons of alcohol are consumed in this state each year! THREE MILLION GALLONS! That breaks down to two gallons for every man, woman, and child in the state! Have you been drinking your share? Or have you been depriving someone else of theirs? Though humorous on the surface, this is no laughing matter. If you have no idea how much alcohol that is you have only to consider the blue water-tower in town here. It would fill that tower 22 times!

The Introductory Teaser

Another means of focusing attention on the topic is the "teaser." It does not reveal the topic precisely, not right away. It keeps it enshrouded in mystery, thus arousing the curiosity of the audience. We have provided the following example:

It has played a role in every war mankind has ever fought. It has also played a role in almost every domestic squabble. It can explain intimacy and interpersonal conflict. It is responsible for corporate mergers and organizational conquests. If fully understood, it can be a tool for building empires or a way of settling sibling rivalry.

This is an introduction to a speech on territoriality and the "human animal." It functions by making vague and sweeping claims about the mysterious, but all-powerful force of proxemics. Members of the audience listen carefully for each new clue that might help them solve the puzzle.

Quotations

Quotations are also often included in introducing a speech. A quotation may enhance credibility if the source is credible, and may elicit common ground if readily recognized. An example is shown below.

Will Rogers never met a man he didn't like. Neither did Gloria. Gloria suffers from a true mental-disorder known as nymphomania.

Sometimes quotations are used to stimulate audience thinking about the central topic of your speech. Such quotations do not have to be from a credible person, they can spring from popular wisdom, which is a highly credible source for many audiences. For instance, one might say:

It has been said that nothing is ever gained without something being lost. Through technology we have gained many things, but what has been the price?

or

Popular wisdom has taught us this about marriage: A man marries hoping that his fiancé won't change and she usually does; A woman marries hoping that her fiancé will change and he usually doesn't.

Stories

Stories are ideal for introductions, providing that they are short. Stories are attention-holding devices in and of themselves, so they are naturally useful introductory tools. We will discuss both the humorous and the dramatic story.

The Humorous Story

Humorous stories are perhaps better suited for informational speeches than they are for persuasive speeches, but there are times when they are useful for the persuader. If you were a Democrat speaking to a Democratic audience then you might begin with a story that "roasts" the

Republicans. Such an introduction would certainly put you on "common ground" with the Democratic group.

Humorous introductions work best when they in some way relate to the specific purpose of the speech. Consider the flaw in the following introduction:

> There was once a young Chinese boy walking down a dark alley with a candle lighting his way. An old and wise man approached the boy and said, "My son, can you tell me where the flame comes from?" The boy thought a long while and finally blew the candle out. Then he looked up at the old man and said, "Now, if you can tell me where it went, I'll tell you where it came from."
>
> The old man hit the boy over the head for being a smart-ass.
>
> This story has nothing to do with my speech today, but I liked it and thought that I'd work it in.

This otherwise charming little story is ruined by the speaker saying that he "wanted to work it in." How much better it would be if it were related to the subject of the talk. Such an introduction might make a wonderful beginning for a talk on philosophy or education. Just "working it in" lacks the artistic touch.

The Dramatic Story

Dramatic stories are imminently suited for the persuasive speech since they can set a serious tone for what will follow. Sometimes describing in detail, and in present tense, the committing of a specific crime can dramatically illustrate a problem that you wish to discuss in your speech. Be careful with these, however, it is easy for them to turn comical on you if you get overly dramatic.

You must make the choices. You may select humor, an anecdote, a quotation, a hypothetical situation, a reference to audience or subject, something startling, some other device or combination of devices. When you select, you will want to refine and perfect that introduction so that you can deliver it with polish. The smoothness of your introduction and its success as a source of audience receptivity will impact on the whole speech. Make the first nine percent count.

CONCLUSIONS

If indeed you make the first nine percent count, your speech will likely flow smoothly to your final words. The conclusion should give the listener a sense of closure and should focus thoughts back on central ideas. The conclusion may summarize, make a final appeal or challenge, or inspire the persuadees to consider or act upon what you have said.

Sometimes, a simple summary serves. This was the case for Mikhail Gorbachev's conclusion to his address to the Communist Party of the Soviet Union's (CPSU) Central Committee:

> Allow me to express confidence that looking ahead to the Twenty-seventh CPSO Congress, the people and party, rallied around the Central Committee, will do everything for our Soviet Motherland to become still more rich and powerful and for the creative force of Socialism to reveal themselves even more fully. (Gorbachev, 1985, p. 208)

Gorbachev's conclusion was simple and encompassed all of his rhetorical intent. Conclusions may be that kind of "wrap up," or they may stand alone as an example of speech artistry. Jesse Jackson's address to the 1984 Democratic National Convention was such a closing:

> Our time has come. Our time has come. Suffering breeds character. Character breeds faith. And in the end, faith will not disappoint.

Our time has come. Our faith, hope, and dreams will prevail. Our time has come. Weeping has endured for the night. And, now joy cometh in the morning.

Our time has come. No graves can hold our body down.

Our time has come. No lie can live forever.

Our time has come. We must leave racial battleground and come to economic common-ground and moral higher ground. America, our time has come.

We've come from disgrace to Amazing Grace, our time has come.

Give me your tired, give me your poor, your huddled masses who yearn to breathe free and come November, there will be a change because our time has come.

Thank you and God bless you.

Reverend Jackson employed repetition, reference to a classic quotation (give me your tired, your poor . . .), and a final inspirational challenge. This is truly an artful finish.

You may choose to refer back to the introduction. This is a common way to give the effect of "bookends." You also cue your audience as to the closure by ending with the same point of focus with which you began.

A conclusion may also be a direct call for action. The call for action may be quite direct as in the case of this sermon conclusion:

Don't you go home tonight and lay your head down to sleep until you write a letter or make a phone call, or visit someone you've been meaning to talk with. "In as much as you have done the least of these, you have done so for me."

Conclusions are not the time for new material which is unrelated to previous points. While it may be polite, the words "thank you" are not novel enough to be used. Also lacking in novelty is the extremely overused "and in conclusion . . ." as a lead-in to the conclusion. The audience should know that the conclusion is coming by the composition of your speech and your style of delivery. You shouldn't have to tell them that the conclusion has arrived.

Make sure that you maintain eye contact and composure until your final words have been received and processed by the audience. As your first sentence should be significant, so should your last sentence be significant. Your final sentence should have a sense of finality about it. Your audience should not have to guess as to whether you are through or not.

SUMMARY

The sequence for planning a speech is body first, introduction second, and conlusion last. The introduction should include any or all of its subgoals: to "grab" the audience's attention, to demonstrate ethos, and to prepare the audience to listen.

There are any number of techniques you might use alone or in combination based upon audience analysis and specific purpose. You might use something startling; a question; a story; a reference to audience, occasion, self, history, or current events; a quotation, or any number of other choices.

A conclusion should provide a sense of finality and refocus thoughts on central ideas. This is your last chance to "wrap up" the speech in a packaged form your audience will accept. Consequently you are looking for a memorable summary, appeal, challenge, request for belief or action, quotation, story, or reference to the introduction, among other possibilities.

The choices for introductions and conclusions are yours, but make them wisely. The choices you make may well determine whether or not you are successful in achieving your specific purpose.

REFERENCES

Alisky, M. (1985, January 15). The U.S.S.R. challenge to the U.S. in Central America. *Vital Speeches of the Day* LI (7) p. 208.

Brooks, W. D. (1978). *Speech Communication* (3rd ed.). Dubuque, IA: Wm. C. Brown Company Publishers.

Cuomo, M. (1985, July 15). Your one life can make a difference. *Vital Speeches of the Day,* LI (19) pp. 581–583.

Gorbachev, M. (1987, April 15). Address to the special plenary meeting of the C.P.S.U. Central Committee. *Vital Speeches of the Day,* LI, (13) pp. 420–422.

Jackson, J. (1984, November 15). The rainbow coalition. *Vital Speeches of the Day,* LI (3) pp. 77–81.

Jeffery, R. C., & Peterson, O. (1983). *Speech: a basic text* (2nd ed.). New York: Harper and Row Publishers.

Lucas, S. E. (1983). *The Art of Public Speaking.* New York: Random House.

Roberts, P. C. (1987, January 15). The unilateral disarmament of the American spirit. *Vital Speeches of the Day,* LIII (7) pp. 212–214.

Trudeau, G. (1987, January 15). The impertinent questions: star wars and skepticism. *Vital Speeches of the Day,* LIII (7) pp. 619–621.

Verderber, R. F. (1979). *The Challenge of Effective Speaking* (4th ed.). Belmont, CA: Wadsworth Publishing Company, Inc.

Visual Support for Persuasive Messages

8

We are a visual culture. With each new generation the visual media seem to take over more of our lives. It is well known that students now in college have spent more time in front of televisions than they have in classrooms. There was a time when novels sold movies. Now it is more likely that movies sell novels. Since John F. Kennedy's election to the presidency in 1960, television has shaped politics far more than politics has shaped television. This extraordinarily powerful medium is becoming even more powerful as Mtv influences the music we hear on radio and the movies we see in the theatre. Even seeing a film in a theatre is something fewer of us are doing because of the ease with which movies can be rented for home viewing.

The point here is not to dredge up old arguments about the goods and ills of television. Every new medium ever created, from the alphabet to the novel to the word processor on which this book was written, has been viciously attacked. The point is to realize how incredibly biased we are toward visual media. Realizing the visual conditioning of our culture helps us understand its inherent need for visual support of oral information.

In the pages that follow we will present some general principles for using visual aids persuasively. You probably know some of this already. Our intention is not to insult your intelligence, but rather, to remind you of what you may have forgotten. Consider this chapter a checklist of principles and strategies that will assist you in making the most persuasive use of visual support.

NOT ALL VISUALS ARE VISUAL AIDS

A man once delivered a speech on the need for stronger enforcement of quarantine laws regarding diseased cattle. He opened his talk by placing a small, toy cow on the table in front of the podium. He held a plastic trough in his hand, filled it with milk, and set it in front of the cow. The speaker pushed the cow's head into the trough and it drank the milk. When it was through drinking, the cow lifted it's head and bellowed a long, mechanical "Mooo." The speaker then moved the trough under the cow, pumped its tail vigorously, and all the milk came out through the utters. The audience loved it. They thought it was the ultimate in recycling products.

From that point he went on to make his speech. When he was through, what do you suppose was the first question the audience asked? Right. "Where did you get that cow?" And subsequent questions were about the cow: "How much does a cow like that cost?" "Could I buy that cow from you? My brother has a birthday soon and I won't have time to find one." His visual only aided him in terms of gaining attention, but from that point it walked all over him and his argument. It set a comical tone for a serious subject. In the end no one cared about stricter enforcement of quarantine laws, though they did care a great deal about the toy cow.

There is no need for a technical definition of visual aids. The name is the definition. Ask yourself, "Are my visuals going to aid my argument or will they detract from it?" "Will they make me more convincing or less so?" The old maxim used by writers is useful here: "When in doubt, leave it out." If you cannot clearly state why you are using the visual, then it is more likely to detract from the speech than it is to aid it.

SPECIAL EFFECTS ALONE DO NOT A SPEECH MAKE

Stephen Spielberg's greatest failure as a director was with the film, "1941." Most critics agree that it had magnificent special effects, but no story. We have all seen films like this, and we have all heard speeches with similar problems. Some speakers present only a slide show, yet fail to add the kind of powerful and insightful commentary that would make the slides truly persuasive. Allowing visuals to "speak for themselves" invites catastrophe for the would-be persuader. They will speak a hundred different messages to a hundred different people. The best persuaders prepare us for the visuals and then tell us how to "see" them and how to "think" about them. In this way the visuals become powerful support for the central theme and purpose.

CONTROL THE RATE AT WHICH THE AUDIENCE PROCESSES YOUR VISUALS

It is unfortunate, but nonetheless true, that audiences will seek diversion whenever they can find it. Seemingly, they will do anything not to pay attention to the speaker. We are all guilty of it. We have all read school newspapers, written letters, doodled, or daydreamed instead of listening to a speech, lecture, or sermon.

Reminding you of this is not intended to make the speaking experience more frightening. Knowledge is power. If you know that an audience can be easily distracted, then you can undertake strategies that will counteract or minimize this problem.

Let us consider for a moment the case of the minister who had a habit of outlining his entire sermon on the black-board behind the pulpit. He often listed 10 major points to be covered. Yet while he was on point 2, many in the congregation were examining points 5 or 8 or 10, wondering what he would say about them. Some were even wondering if he could cover all of that in an hour and let them out in time for the start of the football games. His visual was not an aid. It did not control the rate at which the audience processed the information, and in some cases, the length of it even caused anxiety among the parishioners.

Mark McCormack, author of *What They Don't Teach You at Harvard Business School,* believes that it is best to hide whatever you plan to use as visual support so that the audience will not be distracted. And this even means hiding things outside the room. Closed boxes and covered goods are intriguing mysteries that keep minds occupied (1984, p. 141).

To illustrate further, let us examine two speeches that were similar in thesis and visual support, but vastly different in peruasive effect. Two women gave talks to two separate civic groups. Each spoke on the need for adopting pets from the local animal shelter. The first woman brought out a dog (a lovely Collie) about one minute into her talk. The dog immediately relieved itself on the speaker's platform. The audience laughed uproarously, and though the poor woman went on, she had lost all hope of convincing anybody of anything. The audience was permanently distracted by the dog and the "poop" on stage.

Conversely, the second woman did not even let on that she had any animals with her. An assistant kept them in portable kennels outside the lecture hall. After the woman gave a powerful, 15 minute speech full of convincing anecdotes and statistics, she then brought out first a dog, then a cat, which served as emotional proof for the arguments she had just presented. Her talk was so effective that people had to draw straws to see who would get to adopt the animals right there.

Of course, animals, as Johnny Carson will tell you, are particularly difficult to predict and control. But is this kind of secrecy necessary for all nature of visuals? Absolutely! Many speakers have learned, by bad example, to distribute packets and outlines during their speeches. What happens? The audience reads ahead of the speaker, doodles on the handout, or makes paper airplanes. Even if the audience is exceptionally good about staying with the speaker, there is still a problem. They are looking down rather than at the speaker. Thus, the speaker loses most of his nonverbal channel and his persuasive power is compromised. Save handouts for distribution *after* the speech.

YOUR VISUALS SAY MORE ABOUT YOU THAN YOU SAY ABOUT THEM

Marshall McLuhan, the media guru of the 1960's, wrote a wonderfully fun and insightful book, "The Medium is the Massage." McLuhan helped us see that the media we employ for our messages may be more important than the messages themselves. He reminded us that it is not *what* we say, but *how* we say it that counts.

When Gerald Ford was president he liked using visuals during his televised addresses to the nation. He used beautiful graphs on poster board, which sat on an easel. Though they were colorful and professional in every way, they made him look out-of-date because he was surrounded by the sophisticated graphics of the network news organizations. In a video world, the President of the United States was reduced to resembling a weather man in a small market.

President Reagan, on the other hand, always media smart, does not stand for this. He regularly uses sharp, video graphics during his speeches on the state of the economy. Thus, just the form of his visuals says that he is up-to-date.

Political leaders are not the only ones aware of the medium being the message. Business leaders, too, are painfully aware of it. When surrealistic (MTV-like) advertising began in this country in the 1980's, Lincoln-Mercury was the first automobile manufacturer to follow suit. The President of Lincoln-Mercury explained the move, saying, "In a Spielberg era, if you want your products to look modern, then your ads must look modern too" (Meyer, 1982).

Naturally, these principles carry over into public speaking as well. The quality of your visuals invariably reflects on your credibility as a speaker. Polished, professional-looking visuals say two very important things about you: One, you have thoroughly prepared for your speech so you must know what you are talking about, and two, you cared enough about the audience to bother. Both of these perceptions will build your credibility, and therefore, your persuasive power.

The speaker who says, "I wanted to get this picture blown up, but didn't have the chance," or "I wish I had those graphics here to show you," loses credibility by the ton. The audience says to itself, "Hey, if this guy doesn't care, why should we?"

Naturally, audiences have realistic expectations. Neither student audiences nor your professors expect you to produce video graphics, or even slides for your presentations, though it is always impressive when a student does this. What is realistic to expect is that you should at least have visuals when you need them and that those visuals should demonstrate thoughtful and careful preparation on your part.

Once you graduate and venture out into the cruel world to make your fortune, keep in mind that business and professional audiences have greater expectations concerning the style and quality of visuals you use. Your lack of artistic ability will be solved by Art and Graphics departments that can prepare whatever you want to use, from poster-board drawings to video productions. In big-money presentations, poor visuals and poor use of visuals simply cannot be tolerated.

REMEMBER MURPHY'S LAW

Surely everyone has heard of Murphy's Law by now: "If anything can go wrong, it will." Some believe that Murphy was overly pessimistic. Others see his law as a healthy and realistic proverb by which to live. If you knew, however, that Murphy was a press agent and created his law as a constant reminder to stage producers that they should be ever watchful of potential catastrophe, you would see it as a positive thing. He wanted producers to give thought to the things that could go wrong and take steps to alleviate those potential problems.

In this age of speeches that have multi-media support, Murphy's advice is particularly useful. Ask yourself, "What can possibly go wrong with the visuals I plan to use?" Then work out contingency plans to deal with those problems should they arise. As someone once said, "Success in life is directly related to how well one can execute plan B." At least this way you have a plan B.

Bob Ulery, director of technical marketing for Hewlett-Packard, says that his sales representatives always carry two things in their cars as standard equipment: extension cords and extra projector bulbs. "We don't want to lose thousands of dollars because of a 75 cent bulb," he says.

What are other things that might go wrong? If you use poster board for your visuals, do not roll them up. If you do, they will tend to roll up on you when you place then on the easel. This brings us to the next question. Will there even be an easel? If not, and if you cannot bring your own, you may have to rest your visuals in the chalk tray of the black-board. Since the chalk trays often do not extend far enough to support visuals, they topple to the floor. So you would want to pre-tape the upper backs of the visuals so that they will stay against the black-board.

These are just a few of the things that can go wrong. Your professor will call others to your attention. After all, problems with visual aids are best explained visually. With that in mind, let's move on and examine the various styles of visual support available to you.

MODELS

Mechanical

Models are especially useful for the persuader who deals in abstract concepts. Architects, for instance, face such problems daily. They are constantly trying to persuade potential clients to invest thousands of dollars in complex, two-dimensional drawings with funny numbers and letters all over them. Models can solve this problem. They convert the two-dimensional drawing into a three-dimensional version of reality. Models make the abstract, concrete. Graham Pattinson, a specialist in architectural model building, says that models solve disputes over the interpretations of the drawings, inspire those who might invest in them, and "sell projects, products, processes, and systems" (Pattinson, 1982, p. xiv).

There are times when a mechanical model is indispensable. Nothing else will do. In the wake of the space shuttle explosion, though there was plenty of video footage of the disaster, there was a mad scramble for models of the Challenger. Only by using the model could scientists make the O-ring theory clear to the viewing public. Then, that understanding was transferred to the video replay of the disaster. Once the theory was made convincing on the model of the shuttle, it became convincing on the replay.

Human

Human models are essential for many persuasive efforts. Weight reduction clinics use them in the famous before and after pictures. The clothing industry revolves around the use of people ideally proportioned for the selling of certain styles. Though not often used in persuasive speaking situations, they ought to be. A speaker persuading children to correct poor posture used herself as a model, showing the kids sitting and standing positions that are dangerous to natural growth and development. A young man who was a catalog representative for a small, clothing concern, used male and female friends to model the line of shorts and T-shirts that he wanted the class to buy. He wrote $75.00 worth of orders after that presentation!

SLIDE PROJECTORS

Good slides are powerful support material. Prior to deciding on this medium, however, investigate the room in which you will make your speech. Can you make it dark enough for the slides to be clear in image and bright in color? Will your projector have a remote control system that will enable you to stand in front of the audience? If you answer "no" to either of these questions, then you should not use a slide projector.

If you can answer "yes" to the above questions, then you must next make sure that your slides are developed *for* the speech, and not the speech developed *for* the slides. For instance, you wouldn't want to attempt to sell your ski chalet by using pictures that you took during your fraternity weekend there. The point of those pictures was to capture good times and party prowess, not to sell a chalet. Instead, you would want to take slides with selling the chalet as your main objective. Thus, speed of film, picture angles, and time of day would all figure into your picture-taking strategy. The result would be a far more appropriate and persuasive set of visuals than you would have in adapting your speech to pictures taken previously.

There is no need to show every slide you have. It is this tendency that makes watching your neighbors' "vacation slides" such a brutal experience. They insist on showing you every one of the 637 pictures, bad ones included. Then they explain, at great length, why the pictures are dark and blurred. "But if you look closely," they will say, "you can see the grizzly bear in its den." A little editing is greatly appreciated by your audience and makes your argument tighter and more effective.

Finally, make sure that you load the slides properly (top side down) so that there is no need to interrupt the flow of your speech by having to turn the slides over. Go through some dry runs so that you get used to the order of the slides and can talk about them naturally. Vary the way you introduce each slide. Only the novice, soon to become a bore, introduces each one with, "This is a picture of . . .", which insults the audience and makes them feel as if they're watching Sesame Street.

OVERHEAD PROJECTORS

Think of overhead projectors as electronic chalk boards. They enable you to stand in front of your audience while you project sharp, color-graphics on the screen behind you. Like the chalk board, overheads allow you to draw as you speak; but unlike the chalk board, overheads make it possible for you always to face your audience as you speak. Make sure that you take advantage of this possibility. Do not turn around and look at the image projected on the screen; instead, look at the transparency and use a pencil or a pen to point to those items to which you wish to draw the attention of the audience.

Overheads are one of the favorite media of the business community because of the ease with which transparencies can be made. Most copy stores will now produce them at a rate that is so inexpensive even college students can afford them.

DRAWINGS

Many speakers avoid preparing drawings as visual support because they claim that they have no artistic talent. Whereas you wouldn't want to attempt characatures without proper training, you can produce simple illustrations that help your audience "see" your theoretical argument in practice. Say you wished to convince management that a new floor layout would make the sales staff more productive. With a ruler and magic markers you could help them see the wisdom of your plan, even if it were not drawn to scale. This nature of drawing is more science than art. Anyone with initiative can do it.

MAPS

Maps can be ideal persuasive visuals. They make for "objective" and colorful backgrounds for persuasive messages. A man was attempting to convince doubters that South American Killer Bees could easily migrate as far north as New York City. Following his assertion to that effect, he put up an eight by five foot map of the Western Hemisphere and demonstrated clearly that the Killer Bees already flourished in a latitude in South America that was analogous to New York City's latitude in North America. True, he could have just said that, but his marking the latitudes with a large, red pen imprinted that image, and hence, his argument, in the minds of his audience.

DEMONSTRATIONS

Nothing convinces like a good demonstration. Think of all the things that you have doubted in your life which have been proved to you by means of demonstration. "Show me," you said, and someone did. Perhaps someone claimed that a boiled egg larger than the mouth of a milk bottle could be sucked into the bottle without anyone or anything touching the egg. You said, "impossible," until you learned of the power of a vacuum.

As with all visuals, you need to practice your demonstration a number of times before trying it before an audience. Make sure it works and works all the time. Just as nothing convinces like a demonstration that works, nothing causes greater doubt than one that doesn't. When is the last time you bought a car that wouldn't start?

If the demonstration failing is a possibility and if the presentation is truly important, such as a sales presentation designed to win a large account, then you might consider video-taping the demonstration and showing the video. That way your demonstration works perfectly every time, providing the video equipment works.

If you do a demonstration, try to set it up as much as possible in advance of your speech. Your audience doesn't want to watch you setting up your computer or wok or exercise equipment. When you actually do the demonstration, do not clam up. Talk your audience through it. And whatever kind of visual support you are using, remember not to talk to your visuals; talk to your audience.

Finally, we conclude with some specific suggestions on how to present statistics visually and persuasively.

DISPLAYING STATISTICS

Informational speakers wish to make sure that audiences *understand* their statistics; persuasive speakers wish to make sure that audiences are *influenced* by the argument that their statistics illustrate. Thus, the persuasive speaker should think of his visuals as visual arguments. A good display of a statistical argument should be simple enough for most in the audience to state the argument being made just by looking at it. At worst, visual displays should require the briefest of explanations.

There are at least four popular forms for displaying statistics. It is best to use these forms with most audiences because they have seen them often and can make sense of them easily: the pie graph, the bar graph, the line graph, and the combination line and bar graph.

The Pie Graph

Pie graphs display statistics frozen in time. They do not show historical trends or projections. However, that is the advantage of the pie graph. It is limited to a simple display of who or what has what share of something at a given point in time. Of course, you can use pie graphs to demonstrate share changes over time, but line graphs are better suited for such historical views of data.

The pie graph on the following page shows where the money for running the good ol' U.S. of A. came from in 1987. One does not have to stare at it too long to see that government borrowing to pay its debts is somewhat out of control.

The Line Graph

Line graphs generally illustrate statistical information in a time by quantity format. They function quite well in supporting arguments that concern the increase or decrease of something over time. A line graph might reveal a dramatic rise in divorces over a ten year period. However, line graphs become more persuasive when they are coupled with other line graphs to prove one phenomenon is correlated with another. The two line graphs on the following page illustrate how a speaker might support an argument asserting that cocaine sales and the murder rate are related.

Some line graphs reporting economic data can become incredibly complex. Realize that such graphs require study to understand them. If you cannot explain your graphs in just a sentence or two, they are not appropriate support for oral argument.

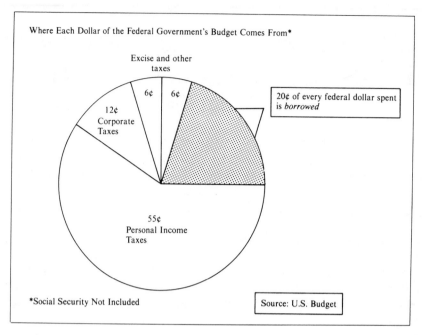

Where Each Dollar of the Federal Government's Budget Comes From*

Excise and other taxes

6¢   6¢

12¢
Corporate
Taxes

20¢ of every federal dollar spent is *borrowed*

55¢
Personal Income
Taxes

*Social Security Not Included

Source: U.S. Budget

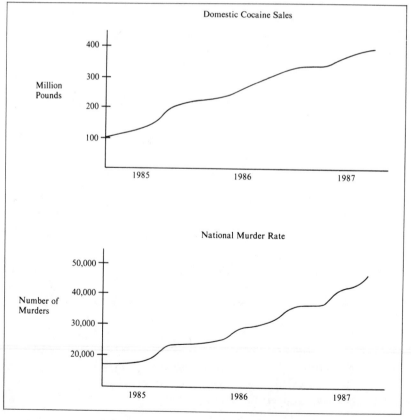

Domestic Cocaine Sales

Million
Pounds

400

300

200

100

1985   1986   1987

National Murder Rate

Number of
Murders

50,000

40,000

30,000

20,000

1985   1986   1987

The Bar Graph

Bar graphs are probably the most popular form for displaying statistics. *USA Today* uses large, colorful bar graphs in every issue. Not only are they easy for an audience to understand, they are also attractive.

Use bar graphs for comparing data gathered on two populations. For instance, bar graphs are ideal for comparing cancer rates between men and women over fifty, or for revealing a disparity in the numbers of male and female nuclear engineering majors. What arguments are made by the following bar graphs?

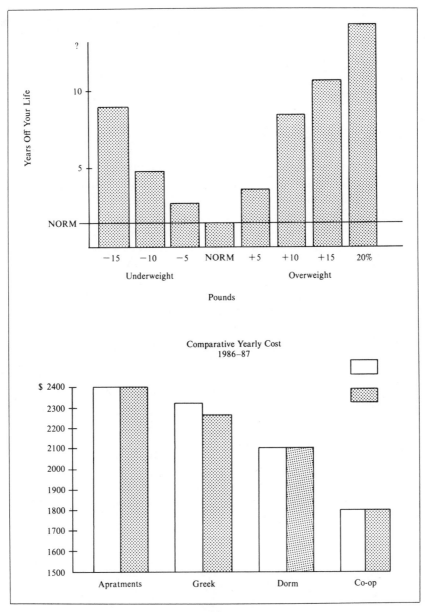

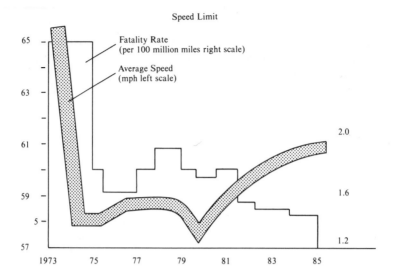

The Combination Bar Graph and Line Graph

This hybrid graph form is one of the more modern, and therefore, impressive and visually attractive means of displaying statistics. It is created by overlaying a line-graph on a bar-graph, which is usually used as a colorful backdrop, creating contrast between the two statistical trends. This visual argues that although there was a correlation between the 55 mph speed limit and loss of life for a few years, the relationship no longer holds. Even though the actual speeds that people drive have been increasing in the last couple of years, highway deaths have continued to drop.

SUMMARY

Since we are a visual culture, we expect to see visual support of speeches. Visuals can add power to an already powerful argument, but they can easily detract from the argument if not prepared and used properly. Remember to ask yourself if your visuals will make you more or less persuasive in deciding whether or not to use them.

You have much to choose from in the way of visual support: models, mechanical and human, slides, overhead projectors, poster-board drawings, and graphics, including pie, line, bar, and bar-line graphs. Whatever you choose, prepare carefully, and practice, practice, practice explaining the visuals and using the medium that you will use to display them.

REFERENCES

Meyer, W. (1982). Three new "big ideas." *Houston Chronicle,* August 31, 4, s. 3.
McCormack, M. (1984). *What they don't teach you at Harvard Business School.* New York: Bantam Books.
Pattinson, G. *A guide to professional architectural and industrial scale model building.* Englewood Cliffs, New Jersey: Prentice-Hall.

Making Language Persuasive

9

Language is our most available medium for persuasion. We carry it in our heads, and hopefully, it rolls effectively off of our tongues when we need it. Yet, even when everything goes right, we have varying degrees of success when we use words to persuade. Why is this so? Why do some people use words more persuasively than we do? Is it because they know more words than we know? No, a large vocabulary alone does not insure persuasive use of words. If such were the case, common people could never have risen to positions of great power in every part of society. Are some people more persuasive by virtue of the life they give to words when they say them? Certainly a dynamic delivery helps, but such a talent alone will not make words persuasive. Making language persuasive requires, among other things, a sensitivity to "how words mean" and how people respond to them. In fact, if you were to examine carefully the most successfully persuasive people and institutions in history, from Demosthenes to Madison Avenue, you would discover that they all have at least three language strategies in common: identifying, labeling, and packaging. It is through the study of these strategies that we can make our own words more persuasive.

IDENTIFYING

The evening news recently aired a special report on the alarming number of white South Africans who were buying firearms. The reporter briefly interviewed a burly, white man who proudly displayed the 12-gauge shotgun that he had just purchased. When asked why he wanted such a powerful weapon, he pumped it once and said, "because 'shotgun' is a language that everyone understands."

Though talking about coercion rather than persuasion, this man tapped into a something that Kenneth Burke, one of the leading persuasion theorists of this century, has been saying for a long time: "You persuade a man only insofar as you can talk his language by speech, gesture, tonality, order, image, attitude, idea, *identifying* your ways with his" (Burke, 1950, p. 55). Burke believes that "language" means more than mere words; it is all symbols, verbal and nonverbal. Hence, we are most vulnerable to the persuasion of one who uses the words we use, speaks with our accent, and dresses as we dress. This is true with one provision: we must perceive such a person as more knowledgeable about the issue in question than we are. Such a provision does not diminish the influence of the other factors Burke has mentioned. For example, how many times have you heard a member of the working-class reject a politician's speech by saying something like this: "He comes down here in his fancy car with his fancy clothes usin' them fancy words tellin' me he

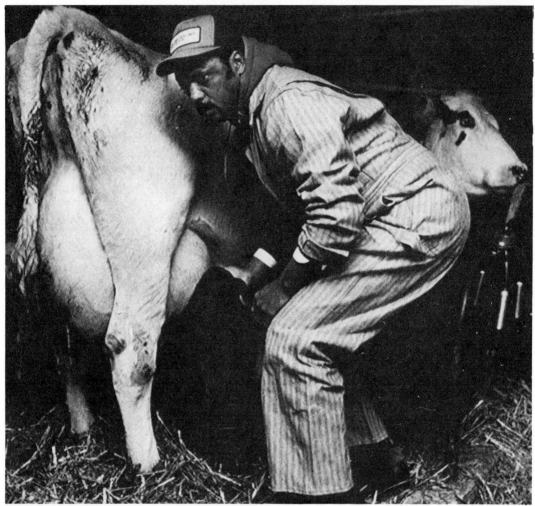

Jesse Jackson "identifies" with Iowa farmers on an early campaign swing through the Midwest. Photo courtesy of AP/Wide World Photos.

understands my problems. What the hell does he know about it?" The politician may actually know a great deal about the problems of the working class. He may indeed be the person most capable of solving the problems. Yet it will make no difference for he will not be heard until he "speaks their language" in some meaningful way. In fact, it is interesting to notice how often people use that phrase at the precise moment that they are persuaded. "Now you're talking my language!" they will say. So it is more than just an expression.

What's a politician to do? He cannot put on a workshirt and wear a hardhat and pretend that he is like his audience. They would see through him in a minute, and the damage to his image would be even greater than the damage suffered for just being "ignorant" of the working-man's life. No, the smart politician gets prominent working-men who speak the language of the working-man, both verbal and nonverbal, to endorse his candidacy. As we pointed out in the chapter on credibility, "It isn't what you say, but who you get to say it" that matters most in persuasion.

Such needs for identification are by no means restricted to the arena of politics. Business leaders, too, must endeavor to identify with employees far below them in order to motivate them. Lee Iacocca was able to save Chrysler from bankruptcy by winning salary concessions from his workers. This he achieved, at least partially, by using the proper language. In his autobiography he wrote, "It is important to talk to people in their own language. If you do it well, they'll say, 'God, he said exactly what I was thinking.' And when they begin to respect you, they'll follow you to the death. The *reason* they're following you is not because you're providing some mysterious leadership. It's because you're following them" (Iacocca, 1984, p. 55).

Madison Avenue has been tremendously successful in selling products by relying on language with which consumers can identify. Just as you are judged as "with it" or "out of it" by the language you use, so advertising is likewise judged. No advertiser today would dare try to sell a Honda scooter by calling it "groovy," but they would and do try to sell it by calling it "outrageous." Such a word is used because it is in vogue in the market they have targeted to sell. Like most things on TV, however, a word or expression will hold on to stardom for only a short time. Soon the word or phrase suffers from overexposure and gets the ax. Such was the fate of "Where's the Beef?" Consequently, most of us remove the worn-out words from our speech and replace them with the new "hot" words, with which advertisers use to identify with us once again. And so it goes.

Identifying with a given audience, will not, in and of itself, persuade that audience to believe what you want them to believe nor to take the actions you want them to take. It is just a starting place, but one that is essential before any communication, and therefore, persuasion, can occur.

How to Use This Perspective

Identifying with the audience through language can be done in two ways. First, if you are a member of the group to which your audience belongs, exploit that advantage. If you are a Texan, speaking the language of Texans ought to be an easy thing to do. "That's obvious," you say, "I don't need a book to tell me that." It may be obvious, but a good number of Texas politicians have lost races because they forgot it. In trying to sound "sophisticated" and "knowledgeable," they spoke the wrong language and were judged "uppity" by the voters.

Similarly, many college students have failed to be persuasive with their peers because they attempted to use unusual or non-peer langauge. A young woman wanted to persuade her classmates that they should always put their full intellectual effort into even the easiest of classes. She spent hours interviewing professors and getting their insights on this problem. What a good idea! Yet, despite her research effort, her speech failed. Her speech suffered from the residue of professorial language and sounded too scholarly. For instance, she said, "Students who pursue true intellectual excellence never register for classes on the basis of weak scholastic criteria." She was not quoting anyone, mind you. These were her words. The students wondered if she were speaking to them or to some imaginary, scholarly audience. How could she have said the same thing in the language of her audience? Perhaps she could have said, "Students who always seek out blow-off courses are getting blow-off degrees." You try. Maybe you can do better.

Identifying with your audience when you are one of them means using words and other symbols that continually remind them that you are one of them. It also means putting their unexpressed thoughts and feelings into their words for them. This does not mean any words, it means their words, what they would say if they could say it. This is the function that many comedians perform for us. When Mark Twain said that he didn't much care for compliments because he was always left feeling that the person doing the complimenting "hadn't said enough," he expressed in those final three words something that every human has felt but has been unable to articulate. It is for this reason that comedians and humorists are quoted so much. They have unique ways of expressing the unexpressable.

Second, suppose you are not a member of the group with which you wish to identify. What do you do then? Certainly you do not try to speak the language and accent of a Southerner when you are not a Southerner yourself. This does not mean that you cannot use some Southern terms, however. When President Reagan was campaigning for his new tax plan in the summer of 1986, he gave a speech to the citizens of Dothan, Alabama. He sprinkled his speech with Southern expressions. At one point he said, "When the special interests up in Washington hear all this good news, they say, 'No,' but the American people, my friends—the people say 'Yes' and 'Hot Darn' " (Hume and Murray, 1986, p. 2). In using "hot darn," Reagan showed his Southern audience that even though he was not one of them, he was willing to try to be. He delighted and complimented them through his efforts to speak their language.

Note that Reagan used a "safe" expression. He knew it would please his audience and that it could not back-fire on him. Stooping to stereotypical images of a population can insult them. A lawyer speaking to the Western Speech Communication Association tried to identify with his audience by saying that he was nervous about speaking in front of people who knew so much about speaking, but that he had been a member of "Toastmasters" (an organization whose chapters consist of people who wish to improve their skills in public speaking), and thought that he would do just fine. Evidently, the lawyer felt that slipping the word "Toastmasters" into his speech would endear him to the Speech Communication professors. It did not. It only demonstrated that he had a simplistic and stereotypical view of a diverse discipline. Had he tried out that introduction on any member of the association prior to his speech, he would have been told that it would have the opposite effect of what he intended. Thus, if you are not sure whether or not you are speaking the language of your audience, get a member of that group to listen to your speech in advance.

Speaking the language of your audience is easy in theory and difficult in practice. Give careful consideration to each word and phrase you plan to use. Ask yourself how the audience might interpret it and how they might respond to it. If you do this well, you will create an environment that will enhance the power of your arguments.

LABELING

How do you rate Haagen-Dazs Ice Cream? Do you consider it one of the world's best ice-creams? What do you think of Forenza clothes? Forenza must be a quality designer since his label is the third best-selling label in sportswear. And what about the famous wine coolers made by Frank Bartles and Ed Jaymes? Theirs is the most popular wine cooler in America.

These products have success in common, and they also share in the fact that they are all successful due to inventive labeling. Not only is Haagen-Dazs not a Swiss ice-cream, it is not even a Swiss word. The Haagen-Dazs label was created for the purpose of sounding foreign, giving the product an appeal it could not get any other way. Forenza clothing is marketed as if a good-looking, gray-haired Italian designer had created them. In fact, there is no Mr. Forenza. He is the convenient fiction of a marketing staff. Bartles & Jaymes, you no doubt know, are two down-home characters that give some "little guy" appeal to a product of Gallo, the wine-making giant (Solomon, 1986).

Bartles & Jaymes Co. Used with permission.

The ethics of such marketing practices are always open to debate, especially for those companies who lose dollars as a result of their competitors' labels. Of course, this is no new thing in advertising. Without straining you could think of similar cases. Betty Crocker and Mrs. Smith's Pies come to mind. The ethics of the practice is not the concern of the moment, however. These were brought to your attention as a means of pointing out the power of words. Words do indeed control how we see and think about the world around us. Haagen-Dazs ice cream might not taste as good to us if it were not for the implied Swiss connection; Forenza clothes probably would not have their romantic allure without the Italian image; and Bartles & Jaymes would be less satisfying if sold as "Gallo's Premium Wine Cooler." Advertisers seem to have the greatest skill in the labeling game. Indeed, it may be that "new" and "improved" and "revolutionary" are the most persuasive words in the English language today.

This process of labeling things starts very early for us humans. When we were children of five, we were already beginning to resent the label of "baby." If someone said, "You can't go, you're still a baby," we resented it. We learned quickly that it was a form of suppression used by our older brothers and sisters to keep us out of their hair. Most of us eventually escaped the label by growing out of it.

Black Americans were suppressed for centuries by a label they could not outgrow—"nigger." It was used by members of the white majority to suppress an entire race. Black students have assured us that their emotional response to the term is so strong that they even object to seeing it used in an academic context such as this. They want the label that has done so much harm banished for good. We risk offending them to point out the tremendous success they have had in driving the word out of common and even private use. Opportunities for blacks have grown as the label has died.

The women's movement, too, has been concerned with doing away with damaging labels. Women in offices all across the country have changed the way male colleagues and bosses view them by insisting that they not call them "girls." When the men protested, saying that they didn't mean harm by it, the women said, "It doesn't matter whether you mean to hurt us or not, the damage is the same. It keeps us down."

In all three cases we have seen how labels play a part in suppressing people of lesser power. If the suppressed wish to make any true advances they have to start with the language that suppresses them. They have to insist that those damaging labels distort reality and that they are not acceptable. It is not an easy road, but it is the only way to affect lasting perceptual changes.

How Words Mean

If we want to understand how labels have such power, we must first understand how words mean. The traditional view of language, and one that many of us were raised on, is that words are containers of meaning. They have a proper use. Did your parents ever say things like this to you: "How many times do I have to tell you!" "Can't you understand plain English!" "Are you deaf?" They were implying that the meaning was right there in the words. All you needed to do was pay attention and you would understand what they meant and act accordingly. Such a perspective relies on *denotative* or dictionary definitions of words. From this point of view the dictionary is the "god" of words. It tells us what they mean and we should use words in compliance with those meanings.

This is not a healthy perspective for persuasion, however. Suppose the football coach of a major university were to praise the president of his institution by saying, "The President's new propaganda campaign has raised a lot of dollars for the football program." The word "propaganda" would certainly seem a strange choice because we may associate the word with "lies," "half-truths," and "communism." Even so, the coach could defend the word by whipping out his dictionary and showing that it simply means "the spreading of information helpful to a cause." Nonetheless, he would be criticized for ignoring the connotative or popular definition of the word. In social influence, what people believe words mean is more important than what the dictionary says they mean. Why all this confusion over connotative and denotative meanings? Language changes in meaning so quickly that dictionaries have a difficult time keeping up with the new ways that people are using words. "Ignorant" does not mean "stupid" (technically), but that distinction is irrelevant to the person who has just been called "ignorant." Therefore, to the persuasive speaker, connotative meanings are more important than denotative meanings.

I. A. Richards was one of the first language theorists to illustrate the ignoarance of relying on denotative definitions of words when precise and persuasive communication is our goal. He believed that meanings are in people, not in words. To illustrate this he created the "Semantic Triangle" or "Triangle of Meaning." The following example may help in understanding the diagram.

When I say, "On my walk to work today I was bitten by a dog," what kind of dog pops into your mind? Focus on that image for a moment. Is it a Poodle, or a Doberman, or is it a German-Shepard? The breed of dog that immediately popped into your mind was dependent upon your personal history with dogs. If you were ever bitten by a dog yourself it might be that you conjured up the image of that particular dog. This process of using a word, in this case "dog," to call to mind the image of a dog when a dog is not physically present, is called abstraction. It is one of our unique human abilities—to think of things that are not physically present. Imagine your predicament if you had to have a dog present to communicate what one was. If your dog were lost, you would not be able to get others to help you find it. In fact, without the power of abstraction, you would not even know that your dog was missing.

As is often the case, our greatest strength is also our greatest weakness. Since we can all imagine a dog without a dog being present, we think of different dogs. The dog you think of may bring to mind happy memories while the dog someone else thinks of may make her afraid all over again. Thus we see that I. A. Richards is right when he says that meanings are in people, not in words. We attach a most individualized meaning to the word dog. This cognitive process is presented in the "Triangle of Meaning" below (Ogden and Richards, 1953, p. 11):

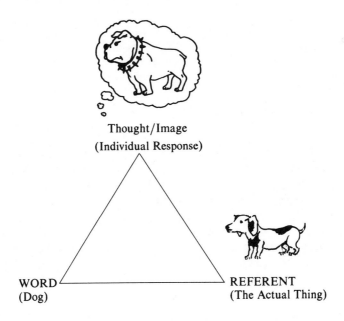

Thought/Image
(Individual Response)

WORD
(Dog)

REFERENT
(The Actual Thing)

Richards believes that our problems with language stem from thinking that everyone shares our very personal "Thought/Image" reaction to a word. This comes from our being taught that words mean things, that they are containers of meaning, and that if we just use them in the right places our messages will be abundantly clear. We have been raised, for the most part, on denotative meanings for words when it is connotative meanings that explain how people relate to the world.

The most significant concept illustrated by the triangle is that words trigger responses in us. "Liver & Onions" may make you salivate or it may make you want to put your hand over your mouth. The response you have is dictated by the good or bad experiences with which you associate Liver & Onions. Just as a whiff of the right perfume or a few notes of a favorite song can bring memories of long ago crashing in, words can trigger similar responses. It is for this reason that labels are so powerful. Haaggen Dazs triggers beautiful Sweden, and Forenza triggers romantic Italy. "Baby" invokes images of helplessness, and "girls" connotes lack of career goals. So, despite the childhood chant, "Sticks and stones may break my bones but names will never hurt me," which we all used as a linguistic shield, we have learned by now that names can do far more than break bones—they can break hearts and souls as well.

"God" and "Devil" Terms

Richard Weaver, in his now classic essay, "Ultimate Terms in Contemporary Rhetoric," has taught us, better than any other modern thinker, that labels disclose what an individual or a society cherishes most. That which is valued most highly is labeled with a "god term," and that which is most threatening to the "god term," becomes a "devil term."

Weaver defines the "god term" as that "expression by which all other expressions are ranked as subordinate. . . ." (Weaver, 1953, p. 212). In the absence of a state-sanctioned religion, non-religious terms rise to the top of the language heirarchy. What might such terms be in modern America?

> . . . If one has to select the one term which in our day carries the greatest blessing, . . . one will not go far wrong in naming "progress." This seems to be the ultimate generator of force flowing down through many links of ancillary terms. If one can "make it stick," it will validate almost anything. It would be difficult to think of any type of person or of any institution which could not be recommended to the public through the enhancing power of this word. A politician is urged upon the voters as a "progressive leader"; a community is proud to style itself "pro-gressive." . . . There is no word whose power to move is more implicitly trusted than "pro-gressive." (Weaver, 1953, p. 212)

Though Weaver published this in 1953, it seems no less true today. When the space shuttle Challenger exploded, President Reagan explained to millions of shocked school children that such tragedies are the price of progress. That somehow justified it. What else have Americans stood for since the Revolutionary War if not progress? Our westward movement and the spirit of "manifest destiny" are neatly concealed in the term.

Closely allied with progress is the god term "Science." You may experiment with this yourself. See how much more persuasive you are when you say things like, "Science has demonstrated clearly . . ." or "Science has taught us . . ." or "Scientists believe. . . ." Of course, you will want to cite specific sources to support your claims. Otherwise, you are claiming that all scientists agree on one issue, which is rarely the case. Still, as Weaver points out, just the word science is so persuasive that slipping it into an argument often makes the argument persuasive, whether it deserves to be or not. Read any issue of the *National Enquirer* and you will discover the ads of charlatans who claim to have potions that can increase your bust size three to four inches in a week; that can give you thick locks of hair on your slick-as-a-billiard-ball-head in a matter of months; that can make you irresistible to the opposite sex overnight. All of these ads include phrases like, "scientifically proven," "tested by scientists," or "recommended by a panel of scientists at one of the world's leading universities." If it works for charlatans, think how powerful it can be when used ethically, for ethical reasons. Imagine how persuasive you can be when you use the science label with arguments that are logical and sound and based on theories tested by scientists you can actually name!

Weaver identifies "fact," and "efficient," and "American" as examples of other god terms. "Facts" are the things that science gives us, nuggets of certainty. Efficiency is something to which we all aspire. We all want goverment, for instance, to work more efficiently. We do not want our tax dollars wasted because of an inefficient beauracracy. If we are striving for efficiency, we are laboring for a good cause. "American" is a god term because we have come to view America "as the goal toward which all creation moves" (Weaver, 1953, p. 218). "American" is linked with progress. It suffered as a god term in the sixties and seventies, but it has enjoyed renewed health in the eighties. Advertisers use the word freely. Many automobile dealers have asked that we "Buy American." Miller even uses it in their beer-promoting jingle: "Miller's made the American Way."

If "Science" and "progress" are god terms, what words are "devil terms"? Words that threaten that which god terms represent are devil terms. "Un-Scientific" and "un-American" are devil terms. How often do you hear a new law protested on the basis of it being "un-American?" "Communism" is a devil term because it threatens the American way of life. The Korean War and the Vietnam War, and most recently, our involvement in Central America, have all been justified on the basis of preventing the spread of "Communism."

More than anything else, Weaver's insights should help you see how language is used to motivate the masses. It should help you protect yourself from spurious claims and arguments whose only substance is in the liberal use of "god" and "devil" terms. If a speaker says that a certain political action is "un-American," you should look beyond the term and ask why it is "un-American." It may be that it is, but the label alone does not make it so.

Euphemisms

Euphemisms are kind labels for cold-hard truths. We probably have more euphemisms for death than anything else. "John passed away" and "Susie's gone to a better world" are two expressions used to soften the impact of death on friends and relatives. One of the most successful and lucrative businesses in this country rests upon the power of a euphemism: "Life Insurance." Actually, it should be "Death Insurance." You are insured against death, not against life. Yet who would want to buy "Death Insurance"?

It appears that euphemisms are rampant in this modern world. They are created to cast a positive light on negative or neutral phenomena. Can you add to this list?

Common Term	Euphemism
Janitor	Sanitation Engineer
Fat	Full-Figured
Stupid	Underachiever
Riot Police	Crowd Managers
Sales Clerk	Sales Consultant
Re-run	Encore Broadcast
Lying	Disinformation
Used Car	Pre-owned Automobile
Handicapped	Exceptional
Salesman	Product Representative
MX missile	Peacekeeper
War Department	Department of Defense
Terrorist	Freedom Fighter
Bombing	Surgical Strike
Retreat	Re-deployment

One of our favorite terms from this list is "consultant." It must be the leading euphemism of the day. Beauticians have become "Styling Consultants" and "Beauty Consultants." Store clerks have become "Sales Consultants." Put the word "consultant" behind any normal title and the result is increased credibility, and likely, higher costs.

In any ongoing debate on great issues, you will find that many of the arguments focus on the accuracy and fairness of the labels used by the opposition. It is an old argument in response to the question, "What shall we name things?" This is illustrated nicely in an address by Senator Henry (Scoop) Jackson. He asserts that it is virtually un-American to claim that "freedom fighter" is a euphemism for "terrorist."

> The idea that one person's 'terrorist' is another's 'freedom fighter' cannot be sanctioned. Freedom fighters or revolutionaries don't blow up buses containing non-combatants; terrorist murderers do. Freedom fighters don't set out to capture and slaughter school children; terrorist murderers do. Freedom fighters don't assassinate innocent businessmen, or hijack and hold hostage innocent men, women, and children: terrorist murderers do. It is a disgrace that democracies would allow the treasured word "freedom" to be associated with acts of terrorists. (Shultz, 1981, p. 675)

Senator Jackson's argument is powerful because it distances freedom fighters and terrorists. This he accomplishes by consistently coupling terrorists with "murderers." Note that the Senator's argument is not only conceptually strong, it is also convincing in its rhythm. Read it aloud and listen to the effect of the construction of the phrases. Each point is a nicely timed jab at the opposition.

On the following page is another example of an argument that takes on the unfairness of labels. This speaker defends the nuclear power industry. He is not a Senator, but rather, a speaker in a freshman-level, persuasive speaking class.

Another problem with nuclear journalism is the use of inflammatory language. We often read and hear about "deadly radiation" or "lethal radioactivity," referring to a hazard that hasn't claimed a single victim in the U.S. for over 15 years. Hubner and Fry, author's of *Total-Body Irradiation: A Historical Review and Follow-Up*, point out that we never hear about "deadly automobiles" or "lethal electricity" which electrocutes 1200 Americans per year. Nor do we hear about "lethal" water that drowns 8,000 Americans each year (Maclaren, 1985).

Dysphemisms

The opposite of a euphemism is a dysphemism, which disorts the common or neutral term in the direction of the negative. If "underachiever" is a euphemism for "stupid," then "moron" would serve as its dysphemism. When social movements go head-to-head it is fascinating to observe that a war between euphemistic and dysphemistic labels is being waged. One of the hottest modern clashes is between those who are pro-abortion and those who are anti-abortion. Study the chart below and see how each side has a euphemistic label for itself and a dysphemistic label for the opposition.

Common Term	Euphemism (Self-Described)	Dysphemism (Opposition-Described)
Anti-Abortion	Pro-Life	Jesus Freaks & Fascists
Pro-Abortion	Pro-Choice	Murderers & Baby Killers

We could make similar charts outlining the positive and negative terms used in any persuasive movement. Why all the need for this language "covering" and "uncovering?" Clearly the pro-abortion group will not survive in the political arena being known as people who *favor* abortion. So they create a euphemistic covering, in this case, "pro-choice," which they feel more accurately reflects their political and moral position. The opposition, conversely, feels that it is their duty not to allow them to get away with this protective, linguistic cover, and thus invent a dysphemistic label that they feel "exposes" the pro-abortionists for what they are. Naturally, this process works both ways.

Polarization

Euphemisms and dysphemisms represent the extremes of language, words that are found at opposite ends of the language spectrum. This is known as polarized language, which allows for only "either/or" choices. "You're either for us or you're against us." "Support Star Wars Research or learn Russian." "You're either part of the solution or you're part of the problem." All of these statements are examples of polarization at work. They aim for emotional rather than rational responses.

Wherever you find a persuasive movement, you will find polarization. Whether it be war or sports or civil rights or business concerns, polarization will flow from the leaders of the movements. Coaches will tell their players that "winning is everything" because they don't write "played hard" in the record books. Business executives will say to their sales representatives, "Either you gross a million in sales this year or you're out for good." Advertisers will have their actor/models use polarization. They will say, "For this baby it's Pennzoil or nothing" and "All my men wear English Leather or they wear nothing at all."

Though polarization is a useful motivational tool, it is good to recognize that it can box people into a a win/lose dichotomy that is unhealthy. Some parents have been known to tell their children that until they achieve a 3.5 GPA in college, they are failures. Even when they bring home a 3.3, their parents will not acknowledge that they "came close." Consequently, many students will quit trying, knowing that their parents will never be pleased. Some will even become suicidal. Only in very few situations in life is polarization accurate. "Either you're pregnant or you're not" is such a case. One cannot be "a little bit" pregnant.

Polarization was fairly and accurately used by Winston Churchill in World War II. He saw the conflict as one of good vs. evil. He fully believed that a victory by Hitler would alter the course of civilization for hundreds of years. He laid out the stakes to his countrymen as follows:

> . . . Upon this battle depends the survival of Christian civilisation. Upon it depends our own British life, and the long continuity of our institutions and our Empire. The whole fury and might of the enemy must very soon be turned against us. Hitler knows that he will have to *break us in this Island or lose the war*. If we can stand up to him, all Europe may be free and the life of the world may move forward into broad, sunlit uplands. But if we fail, then the whole world, including the United States, including all that we have known and cared for, will sink into the abyss of a new Dark Age, made more sinister by the lights of perverted science. Let us therefore brace ourselves to our duties, and so bear ourselves that, if the British Empire and its Commonwealth last for a thousand years, men will still say, "This was our finest hour." (Humes, 1980, p. 189)

In this passage Churchill reveals in graphic terms the dramatically different worlds that will result from winning and losing. Through artistic use of language he creates a polarized vision that is every bit as powerful as the reality he sees.

Now you should be able see the difference between ethical and unethical uses of polarization. Churchill uses polarization to describe a situation that is, in reality, polarized. Claiming that one must "Support Star Wars research or learn Russian" is attributing polarized characteristics to a situation that is far from polarized.

Metaphor

Merely mentioning the word "metaphor" will make some people feel a bit nauseous. It reminds them of hot afternoons in grammar school when their teacher asked them to "explain what the poet means by this metaphor." As a result, say Lakoff and Johnson, authors of *Metaphors We Live By,* most people think of metaphors as a "matter of extraordinary rather than ordinary language" (Lakoff and Johnson, 1980, p. 3). This is not the case. If you communicate at all, you cannot get through the day without using hundreds of metaphors and metaphorical expressions.

Let us first examine just how metaphors work. In simplest terms, metaphors "carry across" meaning from one concept to another. Generally, when a common and literal expression becomes useful in figurative ways, it is used metaphorically. Many such metaphors have come to us from the sport of boxing. Here are a few:

I was saved by the bell.

That was a low blow!

I'm afraid we'll have to throw in the towel.

He's hitting below the belt!

He's down for the count.

We've got them on the ropes now.

So often are these expressions used in a figurative sense that you probably did not realize that they originated as boxing jargon. Yet they are quite useful for "carrying across" meaning from physical to non-physical situations. "Saved by the bell" is often used by students who narrowly escaped having to deliver the speech for which they were unprepared. "Low Blow" is another name for a "cutting remark," which is itself metaphorical.

Our language is so riddled with sports metaphors that we even use baseball jargon to describe the condition of our love lives. "I couldn't get to first base with her," young men are often heard to say. "I struck out" means almost the same thing. We also use baseball jargon to describe the quality of ideas when we say, "You're not even in the ball park" or "Boy are you out in left field!"

In Reagan's weekly radio broadcast of August 23, 1986, he employed an entire set of baseball metaphors to urge the congress to pass the new tax bill without delay. He said: "It's the bottom of the ninth and tax reform is rounding third and heading home. We're about to score the winning run, not just of the game, but of the whole season."

Now you have the hang of how metaphors function in your daily existence. Try to think of other metaphorical families. How many computer metaphors can you think of? What about business metaphors? Spend some time making a list of those you can think of. You might have a great deal of fun with it. Then again, you may not. You may be growing slightly nauseous from all this talk of metaphors. In that case, let us press on. Hang in there. This turbulence will not last long.

To this point we have attempted to demonstrate that metaphors are very much a part of common language. Indeed, communication would be far less inventive and fun without them. They are linguistic visual aids and create powerful images for the mind's eye. It is in this capacity that metaphors are persuasive.

Since metaphors carry across meaning from something we understand to something we do not, then they allow us to color a concept in the way we want it understood. We use metaphors often to label one person in terms of another. If I say that "Gerald Ford is the Rodney Dangerfield of politics" I am doing considerable perceptual damage to Mr. Ford. Some would maintain, however, that Dangerfield is getting the worst of it. Senator Gary Hart, until the Donna Rice fiasco, gained politically from those who said he was "another John Kennedy." You probably create similar metaphors every day when you say "Lisa's the Einstein of Delta Gamma" or "Joel's an up and coming David Letterman." In every case above, one person is being described in terms of another. If the comparison takes, as in the case of the Hart-Kennedy metaphor, it is a persuasive label that is worth millions.

We also use metaphors to describe one situation in terms of another. "NICARAGUA IS SPANISH FOR VIETNAM" is a metaphor seen on bumper- stickers. It is a persuasive metaphor in that it is probably a factor in keeping U.S. troops out of combat in Central America. Ironically, another metaphor, "The Domino Theory," inspired U.S. involvement in South Vietnam. It was believed that Southeast Asian countries were like a line of dominos. If South Vietnam were allowed to fall, then they would all fall in quick succession to communist rule.

Since we talk about the world metaphorically, we think about it metaphorically. We should be careful about this. Countries are not dominos and they do not fall like them. There are far more differences between Nicaragua and Vietnam than there are similarities. Still, such metaphors will persist because they are "visual aids" of the mind. They make it possible for us to "see" what are otherwise vague concepts. When Carol Burnett says that giving birth is like "pulling your upper lip back over your head," it is not only amusing—it is visually impactful. It gives those of us who will never experience the pain of childbearing "an idea" of what it is like. "Kissing a

If your real estate project is coming up short, call us.

In real estate development, things can go haywire in a hurry. Funds dry up. Tenants evaporate. Suppliers don't come through.

We're a big company with the people, tools and resources to put your non-producing assets back on track.

We've got a crack team of workout advisors, backed by Old Stone experts in a dozen related real estate disciplines.

Real estate monitoring and analysis software that no one else has.

Monthly reports that give you the hard facts you need.

And the overall strength of a $4 billion financial institution with more than a century of nationwide real estate experience.

We won't run your business. We'll just take care of your problem property. So you can concentrate on running your business more profitably.

Call us. 1-619-569-5955. Before any more water goes under the bridge.

OLD STONE
REAL ESTATE
SERVICES, INC.

SEATTLE • SAN DIEGO

A subsidiary of the Old Stone Corporation
A diversified financial services company with 137 offices in 25 states.

Advertisers frequently use *visual metaphors* in their ads. Reprinted with permission.

smoker is like kissing an ashtray" is another example of a visually impactful simile (a metaphorical phrase using "like" or "as"). It, too, is persuasive for the smoker and nonsmoker alike because it hits at a visceral level.

In sum, you should be cognizant of the emotional power of metaphors, and, at the same time, sensitive to their logical weaknesses. When you create metaphors for your speeches, make sure that you do not use too many for one idea. Otherwise you might achieve a comic effect when you really want your audience to be emotionally inspired. Metaphors should not call attention to themselves as they do in the following excerpt from a student speech:

> . . . If you want to be a marathoner who is at the top of the heap and the leader of the pack, then the bottom line is this: you've got to work like a dog every day.

The student has made three mistakes here. He has used trite metaphors; he has used too many metaphors, and he has mixed business and nature metaphors. The result is laughter.

If your subject and cause is grand enough, you may be able to use four metaphors in such a short time. You must, however, work toward an emotional intensity and make sure that your audience shares that intensity so that the metaphors will add to the power of your message rather than call attention to themselves. As someone once said, "If your technique is showing, you're not doing it right." Notice how nicely Martin Luther King uses multiple metaphors in an emotional moment of his famous "I have a Dream" speech:

> . . . This is no time to engage in the luxury of cooling off or to take the tranquilizing drug of gradualism. Now is the time to make real the promises of democracy. Now is the time to rise from the dark and desolate valley of segregation to the sunlit path of racial justice. Now is the time to lift our nation from the quick sands of racial injustice to the solid rock of brotherhood. Now is the time to make justice a reality for all of God's children.

If Martin Luther King had used such strongly metaphorical language to push a non-significant and non-emotional issue, it would have seemed silly. Grand language ought to be reserved for grand causes.

PACKAGING

If you were to invent a new product, you would need to create an appealing package to help it sell. The same is true for ideas. Once you have determined just the right words for labeling your ideas, you will then want to package the words in memorable and persuasive ways. There are many well-tested, effective ways to package your words. In this section we will discuss five linguistic packages.

Antithesis

Antithesis packages opposing ideas so that they can be compared and contrasted. In some ways, antithesis allows examination from outside-in and inside-out at the same time. Here are some examples:

> If guns are outlawed, only outlaws will have guns. (Famous Anti-Gun-Control Slogan)
>
> When the going gets tough, the tough get going.
>
> Let us never negotiate out of fear, but let us never fear to negotiate. (John F. Kennedy's Inaugural Address)

The world is divided into peoples that own the government and governments that own the peoples. (Winston Churchill)

You may not get all you pay for in this life, but you will certainly pay for all you get. (Frederick Douglass)

In each case ideas are made more powerful and memorable by the anti-thesis packaging. The subtle effect is that if ideas can be so expressed, they seem to be true. The packaging gives them the ring of truth, whether they are or not.

Repetition

The frequent use of repetition is one way that the speaker differs from the writer. The speaker's audience needs repetition to fully grasp ideas presented orally. Repetition groups ideas, gives them power, and drives them home. When well executed, repetitious phrases virtually force a rythmic delivery on the speaker and appeals to the audience the way music can. Here are some ways that famous speakers have employed repetition effectively:

So let freedom ring from the prodigious hilltops of New Hampshire.
Let freedom ring from the mighty mountains of New York.
Let freedom ring from the heightening Alleghenies of Pennsylvania
Let freedom ring from the curvacious slopes of California.
But not only that.
Let freedom ring from Stone Mountain in Georgia.
Let freedom ring from Lookout Mountain of Tennessee.
Let freedom ring from every hill and molehill of Mississippi, from every mountainside, let freedom ring. (Martin Luther King's "I Have a Dream")

. . . We shall fight on the beaches, we shall fight on the landing grounds, we shall fight in the fields and in the streets, we shall fight in the hills . . . we shall never surrender. . . . (Winston Churchill)

We believe in only the government we need, but we insist on all the government we need.
We believe in a government characterized by fairness and reasonableness . . .
We believe in encouraging the talented. . . . (Mario Cuomo's Keynote Address at the 1984, Democratic Convention)

Parallelism

Closely related to repetition is parallelism. Whereas repetition repeats the same phrases again and again, parallelism repeats key words in slightly different contexts. In this way a reflective energy is maintained between concepts presented in one paragraph. Parallelism, as you can tell, is difficult to grasp by definition. This method of packaging is best learned by imitation. Malcolm X provides this model for you:

Now in speaking like this, it doesn't mean that we're anti-white, but it does mean that we're anti-exploitation, we're anti-degradation, we're anti- oppression. And if the white man doesn't want us to be anti-him, let him stop oppressing and exploiting and degrading us. (Malcolm X's "Ballot or the Bullet" speech)

In the final sentence Malcolm X has used "opressing" and "exploiting" and "degrading" to refer back to "anti-exploitation" and "anti-degradation" and "anti-oppression" in the prior sentence. This is parallelism. It is an elegant and persuasive means of packaging ideas.

Alliteration

Alliteration is created by making several words in a phrase begin with the "same or similar sound." See? We just used alliteration to define it. When used properly in a speech, alliteration will make an idea memorable and rythmic. Use it in moderation, however. Excessive alliteration can be annoying. By examining advertisments and speeches we discovered these cases of alliter-ation:

Tried, Trusted, & True

power your portfolio

California Cooler

Milestone Motorcar

The Daily Diary of the American Dream (The *Wall Street Journal*'s slogan)

My constituency is the desperate, the damned, the disinherited, the disrespected, and the de-spised. (From Jesse Jackson's 1984 Democratic Convention address)

Where is my family?

I thought we were all going camping out in the country. We all left the house together with lots of picnic gear and they even brought me along for the very first time! They didn't bring any of my food, so I thought I'd get to share some of the goodies, too.

We drove and drove and drove. I just love to ride in the car! After an hour or two they stopped in the middle of nowhere and let me out. It looked like a great spot to camp—very woodsy and secluded, nobody would ever bother us here. I waited for everybody else to get out, too, but they just shut the door and drove away.

It's getting late now and I'm starting to get hungry and thirsty. How will they find me if it's dark? When are they coming back for me?

From the heart of

The Humane Society
of the Pikes Peak Region
633 S. 8th St.
Colorado Springs, CO 80901

NON PROFIT
U.S. POSTAGE
PAID
PERMIT NO. 287
COLO. SPGS., CO

There is a message inside for you from Betty White!

If you happen to receive several of these brochures, please pass one on to a friend who also loves animals.

The Humane Society frequently uses personification to encourage people to treat animals with kindness. Used with permission of Phil Arkow and the Humane Society.

Personification

When you attribute human characteristics to non-human entities you are using personification. We probably do this most frequently with our pets, which makes them irreplaceable because it makes us think of them as human, as members of the family. You talk for your cats. When they are curling about your leg in the kitchen, meowing relentlessly, and ignoring the food you just gave them, you say, "He's saying 'I don't want that garbage you just dished out. Get something good in my bowl or I'm out of this dump for good.' " It is the personification of cats, like famous Morris, that has made the cat food industry rich. The names of the cat foods are personified: "buffet dinner," "chicken entree," and "sliced beef in gravy." Now who is that for? Not for cats. Last time we checked they weren't the ones buying the food. Even the shapes of pet foods are personified. Dog food comes in the shape of little steaks and cat food is sometimes shaped like fish. Now who is *that* for? We humans buy pet food on the basis of what looks and sounds good to us.

Personification can be an effective language strategy for causes more serious than the selling of cat food. Political leaders talk about the country as if it were a person: "Drug abuse is a cancer that is killing this country." "Uncle Sam Want's You" was a tremendously successful recruitment poster for the military. It personified the government, and the spirit of the entire country, in the person of Uncle Sam.

SUMMARY

Since langauge is our primary medium for persuasion, we should come to understand its subtle and not so subtle impacts. We persuade by using language with which others can identify, and this means both verbal and nonverbal languages. We persuade and are persuaded by labels, which can control the way we see and think about the world around us, including ourselves. Finally, even the way we package our words, the way we put them together, can determine to what degree we are persuasive.

REFERENCES

Burke, K. (1950). *A rhetoric of motives* New York: Prentice-Hall.
Golden, J. L., Berquist, G. F., & Coleman, E. C. (1983). *The rhetoric of western thought* (3rd ed.) Dubuque, Iowa: Kendall-Hunt Publishing Company.
Humes, J. C. (1980). *Churchill: speaker of the century* Briarcliff Manor, New York: Stein and Day.
Iacocca, L. & Novak, W. (1984). *Iacocca: an autobiography* New York: Bantam Books.
Lakoff, G. & Johnson, M. (1980). *Metaphors we live by* Chicago: The University of Chicago Press.
Maclaren, D. (1985). The nuclear debate. A speech delivered in a basic course in persuasive speaking at Oregon State University.
Ogden, C. K., & Richards, I. A. (1953). *The meaning of meaning* New York: Harcourt, Brace and Company.
Shultz, G. P. (1981). Terrorism: the challenge to the democracies. *Vital speeches of the day*
Solomon, J. (1986, July, 8). Bartles & Jaymes aren't real guys, but you knew that. *The Wall Street Journal.* p. 1.
Weaver, R. (1953). *The ethics of rhetoric* Indiana: Regnery/Gateway.

Speaking Persuasively 10

Has this ever happened to you? You're sitting in an audience listening to a speech that is *almost* interesting or *almost* persuasive when you think to yourself, "What he's saying is interesting, but the way he's saying it is boring me to death!" You are feeling that the speech, as written, is a good one, but that the speaker's weak delivery is detracting from the power of his ideas. We call this *snatching boredom from the jaws of fascination.* Unfortunately, it is a much too common fault. Speakers mistakenly think that all they must do is read or recite their speech and the power of their words or the brilliance of their ideas alone will persuade or motivate the audience. It just isn't so.

George Ticknor, the hard-to-impress publisher had a vastly different reaction when he heard Daniel Webster speak. He recalled, "I was never so excited by public speaking in my life. Three or four times I thought my temples would burst. . . . When I came out I was almost afraid to come near him. It seemed to me that he was like a mount that might not be touched and that burned with fire. I was beside myself, and am so still" (Lodge, 1911, p. 118). Ticknor's description places Webster in that elite category of ideal persuasive speakers, those who can "set logic on fire."

Since it takes decades to develop that level of competence, we will not attempt to transform you into a fire-breathing orator. However, we do hope to help you rise above the level of mediocrity that we first described. With our advice, and your professor's advice and encouragement, and your good attitude, you can make your delivery more persuasive.

We want you to try an experiment for us. Read the following paragraph *aloud* twice. The first time you read it, try to present it as if you were a newscaster. The second time you read it, double your volume and periodically, according to the way you interpret the passage, point your finger at an imaginary audience. Do this in relative privacy so that you won't be hauled away by people in white coats.

> As a nation, our health is at risk. We are, all together, a billion pounds overweight. Our blood pressure is too high; we eat far too much food, and the food we eat is excessively high in fats.

We intentionally selected a rather mundane passage so that we could prove to you that one of the chief differences between informational speaking and persuasive speaking is in styles of delivery. When you read the passage as a newscaster you were informational in tone. However, when you doubled your volume and used gestures to help deliver the "news," you probably became more persuasive in tone. If Dan Rather were to deliver the evening news this way just one time,

he would be accused of "biased reporting" from every corner of the globe. We have used this self-service demonstration to help you see the differences in the delivery styles of informational and persuasive speakers. We do not in any way intend to suggest that there is a systematic correlation between speaking loudly and speaking persuasively. What we do mean to say, however, is that as a persuasive speaker you must be fully involved in your words. When you read the passage the second time you probably felt more persuasive because you were paying attention to the words; you were emphasizing the importance of the words.

Even when you are merely "acting" animated, it is hard for the power of your delivery not to make you feel animated. This principle should be kept foremost in your mind: No audience ever got excited about anything until the speaker got excited about it. For a basic class in persuasive speaking we cannot stress this enough. Over the years getting students to speak persuasively has been our greatest challenge. We know all people have it in them. If your roommate were to wear your favorite shirt without asking permission, and return it to you badly stained, we know that you could speak to him or her in a decidedly persuasive tone. Just let the bank mistakenly charge you for 10 overdraft checks and we bet that you could deliver a most passionate protest to even the president of the bank. Yes, we all have the capacity for the impassioned plea within us, the secret is in learning how to tap into that reservoir and use it to our advantage.

In this chapter, we will try to help you accomplish this. We will proceed in a way that is different from the other chapters, however. This time we will use a question and answer format. We will pose questions that our students have asked us over the years and try to provide you with succinct and useful answers to them.

HOW DO I COPE WITH THE FEAR OF SPEAKING?

First let us say that the fear of speaking in public is a fear that is experienced by virtually everyone. A survey on "What are Americans Afraid Of?" (1971) discovered that fear of public speaking was the number one fear of Americans. It surpassed fear of heights and fear of snakes, even fear of death itself. Think of what that means. Many people would rather *die* than give a speech. Such an extreme position seems irrational because we know of no one who has died from giving a speech, though we do know of audiences who wish some speakers would have. We make this little joke to highlight one of the major causes of speech anxiety, fear of rejection. No one

wants to be rejected, or laughed at, or embarrassed. Consequently, people avoid such potential embarrassment by avoiding speaking in public. It is sad that many of these same people are avoiding advancing in their careers and in personal confidence because they cannot overcome such a common apprehension. In fact, it was not long ago that one of your authors received a telephone call from a group who wanted him to speak on "Maintaining Power in Office Politics." When he suggested to this group, consisting primarily of mid-level, corporate administrators, that they should get a speaker who "worked in the corporate trenches," he was astonished to learn that they had found four or five people who claimed to have a great deal to say but refused the opportunity to say it because they were "afraid of speaking to groups." We wondered how many of these mid-level administrators were stuck in a mid-level position because they had never overcome their speech anxiety. So that you will not be doomed to the same fate, we would like to give you some ways of learning to cope with and even conquer your speech anxiety.

Beginner's Jitters

Speech anxiety is composed mainly of beginner's jitters. The first time we do anything new, especially if we do it in public, we experience beginner's jitters. The first time you ever went dancing you probably felt tremendous anxiety when you got out on the floor. You felt that you didn't dance well and that everyone was noticing that and pointing out that fact to everyone else. Many beginning dancers cope with this anxiety by drinking a good deal, which inhibits their embarrassment, or at least postpones it until the next day. Speakers, to the disappointment of many, do not have the same option, although there are plenty of amusing stories about speakers who have tried it. The very thing that inhibits the anxiety inhibits presence of mind and verbal fluency as well. Consequently, speakers must learn to master their anxiety and turn it into positive energy.

When you are before an audience, the pounding heart and the sweat-soaked palms and vibrating knees tell you that the age-old "fight or flight" syndrome has kicked in. Adrenalin is pumping through your body, and in truly dangerous situations, you would use that surge of energy to escape the danger. In speaking, however, you can't consume that energy by running away. You have to stay where you are and give a speech! Consequently, you must find ways to control this excess energy rather than letting it control you.

The best way to conquer most fears is to do exactly that which you are afraid to do. You may remember the fear you felt as a child when you wanted to jump off of the high diving board. You stood up there slightly teetering in the cool wind and staring at the image of the drain far, far below. Finally, you jumped (or were pushed), and your fear of the high diving board dissipated in about 2.3 seconds. Chances are you shot out of the water and raced to do it again. We suggest that the same is true for public speaking. We cannot remove the impact of beginner's jitters for you. The only way can get over it is to stop being a beginner. So jump in. The water's fine. You will find nothing in this world (except for sex perhaps) that is as thrilling as delivering a speech that truly influences or motivates or inspires a crowd.

Now that we have told you that some anxiety is inevitable and that there is no magic pill to negate its effects, we wish to make some suggestions about how you can at least reduce the effects of anxiety.

The Audience Is on Your Side

Realize that the audience is on your side. Too many speakers view the audience as an adversary, a mistake-hungry monster watching carefully for any error on which it might pounce. If you will think back over your own experiences as an audience member, you will see this "audience as adversary" notion for what it is—an unwarranted paranoia.

When you hear a speaker tell a joke that fails, doesn't it make you nervous and uncomfortable *for him?* This is because you empathize with him. A little of every audience member shares the platform with the speaker. From this you should be able to see that audiences *pull for* speakers and generally wish them well. The reason for this is simple: audiences don't like to be made uncomfortable by a failing speaker. To put it another way, when is the last time that you attended a lecture and remarked to a friend beforehand, "I hope this woman is terrible. I hope she's boring as hell!" When is the last time you walked to class and said to yourself, "Please, God, make Professor Manuto dull as dirt today. I'd really like to waste an hour of my life!" Of course, you don't do that, and neither does 99% of any audience. They pull for you. They want you to be interesting and inspiring. Even if the audience disagrees with your position, most people still would like for you to be worth listening to, to challenge their thinking. The positive bond between audience and speaker is real. Never forget that they are on your side in terms of wanting you to speak well.

In considering your present audience of your peers, please recognize that it is at once one of the most sympathetic groups and one of the toughest groups you will ever address. It is a sympathetic group because everyone there must deliver speeches, too. You won't find many hecklers in a college speech class, for this reason. On the other hand, your audience can be a tough one in that its members spend all day listening to lectures. Thus, as any teacher can tell you, you must speak in an animated style if you hope to gain and maintain their attention. Audiences outside the university spend so little of their time listening to formal speeches that they often bathe the speaker in warm affection. It can be like speaking to an audience of grandmothers.

Reducing Uncertainties

Try to reduce any uncertainties that trouble you. Some speakers begin worrying about their speeches days before they deliver them. They allow their fears to overcome them and dream up elaborate ways that things can go wrong. They ask: "What if the audience is too large for the

auditorium or the auditorium is too large for the audience?" "What if it's too hot?" "What if my projector bulb burns out?" "What if I accidently shuffle my notes and can't find my place?" "What if I trip on my way to the podium?"

Unrealistic fears spring from realistic ones. So concentrate on those things that you can control and work out solutions for those things that *can* go wrong. If the audience is too large for the auditorium, consider it a positive thing. Packed-in groups are much easier to motivate than one's that are spread out. Adolph Hitler regularly overbooked auditoriums because he wanted the audience to feel "as one." If the opposite fear is your concern, then rope off half of the auditorium so that the audience will be closer and tighter. If you fear that a projector bulb will burn out, put in a new one just prior to your speech and take along an extra one just in case. If you fear that the room in which you plan to speak might be too hot, go to that room at the time of day you plan to speak and see if it's too hot. If it is, try opening windows or pulling blinds to adjust the temperature. If that doesn't work, try to change rooms. You get the idea. If the fear of the unknown bothers you, then reduce the chances of unknown things occuring and you will reduce your pre-speech anxiety.

Isometrics

Use isometrics to help reduce pre-speech anxiety. It's five minutes before you speak and the butterflies are beginning to circle. You feel that nervous energy making your legs bounce slightly on the chair. You keep your palms dry by rubbing them vigorously up and down your pant legs. Now is the time to use isometric exercises. Push your palms together and put the whole weight of your arms into them. Push your feet into the floor and hold them there. Breathe slowly and deeply. By so doing you will consume a good portion of that nervous energy.

If this procedure does not work for you, take faith in the knowledge that, for most people, anxiety dissipates quickly once they begin to speak.

Move around when you speak. Since anxiety is best reduced by physical exertion, move around when you speak, but have reasons for moving. This serves not only to reduce anxiety, but also to gain and maintain the attention of the audience. We humans are always interested in that which moves. Just watch how a student entering class late will invariably snatch the attention away from the professor. This is a valuable lesson to lock into your mind. A moving speaker generally holds interest better than one who stands perfectly still.

Do not, however, run around like John Madden in a Lite-beer commercial. Controlled movement is the objective here. Walk over to the left side of the room to make a point. Stand still right there until you have completed that point, and then move. You ought to use movement to symbolically reflect transitions within the speech.

Talk to individuals rather than masses. One source of speech anxiety is in the number of people being addressed. Somehow, an audience of five-hundred is more frightening than an audience of fifty. Try not to think of any audience as "a mass of people." Think of the audience as a collection of individuals, which is what an audience is. Since each person processes the information through his or her own eyes and ears, talk to individuals. And talk to individuals who give you positive feedback. Ignore those who give you negative feedback. No matter how talented a speaker you are, there will always be those people that you cannot reach, so ignore them. Select attentive faces in the crowd and carry on a conversation with them. Talk with John for a minute, and then talk with Andre. Skip Pam, since she's not listening, and talk with Karen instead. If you do this well you will reduce your anxiety and increase your persuasiveness at the same time.

Some Anxiety Is Good

Recognize that some anxiety is good. We are in some ways sad to tell you that speech anxiety never really goes away, no matter how much experience you have. However, what does happen is that you learn to manage it. Through exposure to anxiety, you eventually inoculate yourself against its extreme effects.

A few years ago Johnny Carson strapped a heart monitor to his chest just before he went on stage to deliver his monologue. This seasoned professional averaged 120 beats per minute during his performance, which is about the rate he would achieve doing a slow jog. So you see, even tremendously experienced speakers have a heightened physiological response to the speech situation. They have simply learned to control it and even ignore it when necessary.

Our belief is that the only thing you have to fear is in having no fear. Whenever you feel no anxiety at all before a speech, then you are in the position of the athletic team that gets cocky before the big game and gets "blown out" by a lesser school because they have no intensity. If you are perfectly calm prior to speaking, chances are you will be "flat" when you do speak.

ISN'T IT TRUE THAT GREAT SPEAKERS ARE BORN AND NOT MADE?

This has been a hotly contested issue since antiquity. We believe that the truly great speakers probably were born with "something extra" that makes them tower above the rest of us in ability. We also believe that their talent had to be nurtured, that they had to study the art and accept the coaching of someone who was intimately familiar with the complex process of persuasion, or they never would have earned such recognition.

No runner, no matter how naturally gifted, ever strolled onto an Olympic track and walked away with the gold medal on his or her natural talent alone. Natural gifts require expert direction in order to get the greatest good out of them. Thus, it is our belief that the potentially finest writers have never picked up a pen and the most gifted composers have never played an instrument and the most persuasive speakers, people that have the negotiation skills to do away forever with this nuclear umbrella, could well be out herding sheep in Montana.

Our point here is that people who say that "great speakers are born and not made" often use the phrase as an excuse not to try or train. We could say this about anything: "Aren't great runners born and not made?" "Aren't great mothers born and not made?" "Aren't great lovers born and not made?" You may not ever be one of the premier orators in the world, but you will never know the extent of your talent until you try. Besides, most of us simply want to push our talents to their natural limits, to be the best we can be.

Select any famous speaker you like and study that speaker's life. You will discover that each one, during his or her formative years, was exposed to especially fine speaking and had many opportunities to practice speaking. Abraham Lincoln studied the speeches of Cicero and spoke to field hands from a stump. Martin Luther King, Jr. was influenced by the rhythmical cadences of Southern Baptist Preaching. His father was a minister and so was he. So he had models and training and practice prior to delivering his finest speeches. Barbara Jordan also witnessed emotionally powerful Southern preaching and honed her persuasive skills in high school and college debate. No one ever became a truly accomplished orator without extensive training and practice, regardless of his or her natural gifts.

As a conclusion to this answer, we would like to tell you the true story of Demosthenes, a kind of Rocky Balboa of ancient Greece. Demosthenes' father made his fortune as a defense contractor. He was a sword manufacturer. When he died, Demosthenes was just a boy and could not prevent his relatives from robbing his family of the fortune his father had made. When he was old enough, Demosthenes took his relatives to court to win back what was rightfully his. Sadly, his weak voice and severe lisp only entertained the jury. He was laughed out of court.

His spirit crushed, Demosthenes sought the aid of a master teacher. He shaved his head and went into isolation and intense training. For months he worked on shaping his mind and overcoming his lisp and building his body. He ran up steep hills carrying boulders in a sling on his back to increase his lung capacity, and therefore, his ability to project his voice. He spent long hours on the beach where he put pebbles in his mouth and learned to speak clearly and distinctly while projecting his voice out over the crashing waves. (He thought about drinking raw eggs and chasing chickens but he dismissed the idea as ahead of its time).

When his master judged him ready, he returned to court, and this time, he annihilated his relatives and won back that which rightfully belonged to his family.

Demosthenes' victory of nurture over nature should give us all encouragement. His training helped him to become one of the leading statesmen of the ancient world, as well as one of the greatest orators in the history of the world. Much later in life (in Demosthenes II), he delivered "On the Crown," which is still regarded by more than a few critics as the most brilliant speech ever delivered.

Considering all that Demosthenes did to overcome his natural deficiencies, it should come as no surprise that when he was asked to name the three things that a persuasive speaker should work on, he replied, "Delivery, delivery, delivery!"

CAN I BE PERSUASIVE WITHOUT A GOOD AND STRONG VOICE?

Absolutely. Sincerity and concern for the audience are both more important than a "good and strong" voice. To use a crude analogy, consider the singing of Bruce Springsteen. We doubt that many musicians would say that he has a "technically fine" voice. Yet that doesn't matter to us. His energy and enthusiasm and concern for his fans overpowers any "technical" defeciency that he might have. We react to speakers in the same way. If they have accents or slight speech impediments (such as Henry Kissinger or Barabara Walters) we don't care as long as we can understand them and believe that they are being honest and sincere. When it comes to persuasive speaking, nothing can take the place of sincerity, providing that the sincerity is communicated.

WHAT DO I DO WITH MY HANDS?

It's odd that we never worry about our hands much until we begin to make speeches. Suddenly our arms and hands can become alien creatures at our sides, capable of committing atrocious acts to us or to the people on the front row. The other possibility is that they might lay limp at our sides and not move when we want them to.

The meaning of any communicator's message is at least 65 percent nonverbal. Persuasive speakers cannot allow the nonverbal channel to be wasted. They cannot allow their hands either to run amuck or to constantly lay lifeless at their sides.

Nonverbal Communication experts tell us that we use *emblems* and *illustrators,* among other things, to communicate nonverbally. Emblems are "nonverbal acts that can be accurately translated into words" (Mehrabian, 1981, p. 4). Speakers should use emblems to identify with audiences and to assure them that all is well, or to assure them that all is not well, to excite them and to pump them up. The classic "thumbs-up" sign assures audiences that "everything is okay," whereas the "thumbs-down" sign implies disapproval. The raised and clenched fist has long been an emblem that signifies "power."

Illustrators may be more useful to persuasive speakers because they "serve the function of emphasis" (Mehrabian, p. 4.). There are two kinds of illustrators, descriptive illustrators and stress illustrators. Descriptive illustrators are what many people insist on using when they carry on a conversation. When they say, "I can't talk without my hands," they mean that they cannot talk without descriptive illustrators to give added meaning to their words. Fishermen who say "that baby must have been this long" invariably use a descriptive illustrator to provide a visual picture of the lie. Persuasive speakers often use descriptive illustrators to explain that a situation is unfair or injust. To do this they use their hands as symbolic scales, placing one a good deal higher than the other.

Stress illustrators are used to emphasize certain words and to direct the rate of the delivery of words. Speakers may pound on the podium, not only to stress their point, but to direct the rhythmical delivery of their words in the same way that the director of an orchestra controls the rate at which the musicians play.

We suggest that you try to use some emblems and illustrators when you speak. Do not, however, go overboard with such nonverbal tools. Excessive use of these devices can only make you appear superficial.

DON'T I HAVE TO PUT ON AN ACT TO BE PERSUASIVE

No. As we pointed out earlier, sincerety is essential. Granted, some speakers feel that if they are to become properly animated they must become someone they are not. We are not asking you to do this. We ask only that you amplify your own personality. The advice of the famous preacher, Henry Ward Beecher, is useful here. He said that the speaker should deliver his speech to his audience in a way that allows him "to bring his personality to bear upon them" (Beecher, 1872, p. 143). So, project a polished and animated version of your natural self.

MAY I USE NOTES?

Informational speakers can get away with notes more than persuasive speakers can. Persuasive speakers should try to keep the use of notes to an absolute minimum. Why? Because audiences feel that when you are relying heavily on notes you are not speaking from the heart. And if you are speaking from a manuscript your delivery is often bland and lifeless.

If you must use notes, rely only on small, unobtrusive note cards on which you write key words that are associated with key points that you wish to make.

SHOULD I MEMORIZE MY SPEECH?

Absolutely not. If you memorize a speech that is 2000 words long, all you have done is given yourself 2000 chances to forget. Since memory is frequently locked into a sequence, if you forget one word, you cannot go on without it. Memorization causes excessive and needless anxiety.

Memorization destroys delivery, too. When you hear a memorized speech being delivered what you hear is a speaker *saying words,* but not *meaning* words. If you watch such speakers carefully you can see them recalling words, but not the images that the words stand for. To become an effective speaker you must learn to see the images that you are describing as you describe them.

We suggest that you use an extemporaneous, conversational style of delivery. An extemporaneous style is one that is planned, but not memorized. If you were to give your speech fifty times, each time you would present it a little differently, but the same basic ideas would be communicated.

We have noticed a curiosity about the delivery styles of some of our students over the years. Some speakers will be monotone and relatively lifeless when delivering their speeches, but will transform into forceful speakers once they are asked a question. This happens, we believe, because some speakers believe that they are imposing on their audiences just by speaking to them. Since they think that no one wants to listen to them they rush through their speeches like they're doing Evelyn Wood out loud. Once they are asked a question, however, they come to life because *someone genuinely wants to know something*. If you have a similar attitude, just prior to your talk, imagine that three or four people in the audience have asked you a question to which your speech is the answer. This should improve the quality of your delivery. You only impose on your audience when you begin to act like you're imposing.

REFERENCES

Beecher, H. W. (1872). *Yale lectures on preaching*. New York: J. B. Ford. As cited in Robert Oliver's *History of public speaking in America*. p. 376.
Bruskin Associates. (1971). *What are Americans Afraid Of?* (No. 53) The Bruskin Report.
Lodge, H. C. (1911). *Daniel Webster*. Boston: Houghton Mifflin. As cited in Robert Oliver's *History of public speaking in America*. p. 143.
Mehrabian, A. (1981). *Silent messages*. Los Angeles: Wadsworth Publishing Company.

Argumentation
and Debate

11

"Look, this isn't an argument, it's just contradiction"
"No it isn't"
"Yes it is!"

Monty Python's Flying Circus

It's hard to imagine a day without argument. We are inundated with opportunities for informal argument day to day. Does a college student have the right to financial support from parents while in school? Should there be enough money provided by parents to 'party properly?' Is this term paper really deserving of a 'C?' Should opposite sex friends live together outside of marriage? Formal arguments abound in a democracy. We hear such issues as follow discussed formally and informally. Should Oregon decriminalize marijuana? Should the United States negotiate a bilateral nuclear freeze with the Soviet Union? Should the Equal Rights Amendment be reintroduced? Is privacy a Constitutional right?

In each example (above) of potential arguments, claim is made by those adhering to one side of an argument or the other. One of you may Claim that privacy is a Constitutional right, another may Claim that it is not. Each of you would probably attempt to validate your claims by argumentation. *"Argumentation is the process of advancing, supporting, modifying, and criticizing claims"* so that appropriate decision makers may render a decision (Rieke & Sillars, 1984, p. 5).

The terms argumentation and debate are often used in tandem. This is because debate is one of the most popular forms of argumentation. Debates, in the most formal sense, are governed by a great many rules governing how to validate claims, offer evidence, and establish a debate case for one side or another of an issue. Debate is taught in high school and college and practiced as a competitive activity because students learn: how to do research, how to evaluate evidence, how to take notes, how to distinguish between essential and non-essential details, and how to listen effectively to others (Ellis & Parro, 1970). It is hoped that you will gain or sharpen some of these skills through classroom exercises in argumentation.

Argumentation has its roots in ancient Greece. The *Rhetoric* of Aristotle discusses three modes of persuasive appeal. The three are ethos (credibility), pathos (emotional appeal), and logos (logical appeal). In the *Rhetoric* the weakness is that the elements have been labeled, but not explained in terms of how those elements lead to persuasive influence (Scheidel, 1967).

Argumentation differs from other forms of contemporary persuasion in that logic is emphasized. In most persuasive messages, there will be an emphasis on psychological suggestion and motive appeals; but argumentation de-emphasizes emotional proof in favor of logical proof. The logic emphasis is NOT because of its persuasive quality, rather logic is emphasized because *argument, properly engaged, is the basis for rational decision making.* We should think of argumentative or debate speaking as having the overall goal of confronting decision makers with choice, and the reasoning behind why a given choice should be made.

ADVANCING AND SUPPORTING CLAIMS

Preparing an argumentative speech is very much like preparing any other message. However, certain special knowledge and analyses are required. First, one must have knowledge of and analyze the *topic* being argued. Second, one must generate and support arguments, requiring knowledge and analysis of *evidence* and *reasoning.*

Topic Analysis

Argumentation requires some sort of statement as to what is being argued. In formal debate, the topic would be stated on a proposition or resolution. In less formal debating situations, it is still advisable to generate such a statement. Examples of debate propositions are listed below.

1. Resolved, that a persuasion class should be required of every student earning a degree at a four-year college.
2. Resolved, that the NCAA should adopt a drug screening program for athletes.
3. Resolved, that the United States should withdraw from the N.A.T.O. alliance.
4. Resolved, that privacy is our most fundamental constitutional right.
5. Resolved, that baseball is a sport for sophisticated fans.
6. Resolved, that Fred Jones is guilty of rape.
7. Resolved, that rock and roll is better music than country and western.
8. Resolved, that leisure time is critical to the average college student's welfare.
9. Resolved, that arms shipments to Nicaraguan contras are morally just.

In the case of each resolution above, one side of the debate would be in agreement with the stated resolution, and the other side would be in disagreement with the stated resolution. If you examine the nine statements above carefully, you will see different points of contention. The nine statements reflect the three kinds of resolutions. The first three examples (numbers 1–3) are *proposition of policy,* which set up an argument based upon the desirability of doing something differently than the way things are currently done.

Propositions of policy contain the word "should," and those arguing for such propositions would be speaking for the desirability of a change from the present system (Ellis & Parro, 1970).

The second three resolutions (numbers 4–6) are *propositions of fact.* Those arguing for a proposition of fact would be defending the truth of the statement. Such propositions are debatable if they have not been settled (Ellis & Parro, 1970). It would be useless to argue the height of Mount St. Helens, since it can be measured to determine its height (of course, that height changes occasionally).

Resolution statements seven, eight, and nine are *propositions of value*. Those arguing for a proposition of value would be defending a view that something is "good, virtuous, proper, admirable, or better than something else (Ellis & Parro, 1970, p. 9)."

Your first step in analysis should be to identify where you stand and what kind of proposition you will be debating: fact, value, or policy. Obviously, for every person arguing for a resolution, there is an opposing point of view which argues against the resolution (Note: this is *not* true of example 7, which is a true statement). A good statement of a topic contains controversy, focuses upon a single idea, and does not use value-laden terms. This allows for both sides to advocate legitimate points of view. Begin, then, by writing out a statement of the topic. For example, if two sides are arguing the issue of whether or not to build a new recreational facility in their hometown of Hebron, Indiana, the resolution might be stated in this way:

RESOLVED, THAT THE TOWN OF HEBRON SHOULD BUILD A NEW PARK.

In a debate, it is required that speakers clearly state the topic just as it is worded above. However, debate which is not rigidly bound by rules and structure does not require beginning with the words, "Resolved, that. . . ." The purpose for stating a proposition is to create a clear and accurate identification of the subject to be debated so as to eliminate confusion, wasted time, and ill will and to ascertain central issues (Thompson, 1971). As long as the goal of ascertaining central issues is met, the statement of the debate topic is correct.

Once you have identified the topic, you begin preliminary analysis to building a case. Preliminary analysis involves extensive reading and/or discussion of material with others. You are seeking in preliminary analysis to discover key issues on which to build a case. You want to:

- find the causes for the topic being debated
- discover the history and background of the problem
- define any terms which must be clear for a good debate
- set the goals for your side
- discover the vital issues which each side will argue (Ellis & Parro, 1970)

You will want to find causes for topics being debated because you will discover circumstances which may affect your argument. In the case of all propositions of policy, and most propositions of value or fact, there have been events which caused this topic to be a focus of public attention. Such foci generally generate discussion, news and magazine articles, and perhaps books for which you will want to look to learn more about the topic.

Let us suppose, for example, you were debating the topic: "Resolved, that the United States and the Soviet Union should negotiate a mutually verifiable nuclear arms reduction treaty." The probable cause for debating such a topic might be that President Reagan and Premier Gorbachev have been discussing the possibility of meeting on this topic. With a topic of this magnitude, you will find a virtually limitless supply of articles in newspapers and magazines. You would also want to identify experts who have spoken, taught, and written on the subject of strategic nuclear defense (Dr. Henry Kissinger, for example), and seek out their writings.

The history and background of a problem gives you keys as to what has been tried as a solution or answer to the problem. History and background may also reveal where you may find evidence *for or against* a topic. If we again use our topic of nuclear arms limitation, you would want to examine events such as Hiroshima, and the Cuban missile crisis as well as military and political journals on the destructive force of nuclear weapons, past nuclear limitation treaties, who has broken what treaty when, et cetera.

Definition of terms also gives you more insight into what the topic is really all about. In fact, the question: "What does this mean?" is a key question in any kind of thorough analysis. When we speak of nuclear arms, for instance, do we mean the nuclear warhead itself, or do we include the delivery system? Is a B-1 bomber a "nuclear arm?" What about a Howitzer 155 artillery piece, which can deliver a conventional weapon or a tactical nuclear warhead equally well? The issue of "mutual verification" also needs defining. How will we confirm that the other side is destroying warheads or stopped making new ones? Definition of terms saves a waste of time in the debate. Otherwise, you spend too much time in quibbling over what words actually mean.

Setting the goals for your side helps you better enumerate the arguments for your case. With our nuclear arms topic, the goal might be:

TO REDUCE THE LIKELIHOOD OF A NUCLEAR WAR.

Probably, both sides could agree to the above goal. As you will see, there may be arguments on either side of this propositon regarding how to meet this goal with the most success. By setting a goal and stating it clearly, the task of finding the competing arguments is made easier. If our goal is reducing the likelihood of nuclear war, the advantage of arms limitation argreements might be built on the idea that because we have the capacity to obliterate all life on earth, and reduction in arms makes averting the nuclear holocaust a more likely future. On the other hand, the opposing side may argue that the threat of destruction by the superpowers is what deters nuclear war. Therefore, the opposing side would argue, we don't want to limit nuclear arms because the Soviets might not hold back on the use of nuclear warheads if they thought they could win such a war. A competing side might offer a "counter-goal" in which case the debate may become a question of who has the better goal. For instance, a counter-goal might be:

TO MAINTAIN A NUCLEAR DETERRENT SO AS TO AVOID A CONVEN-TIONAL WARFARE ATTACK BY THE SOVIETS IN EUROPE. . . .

OR

TO ASSURE AMERICA'S VICTORY IN AN ALL-OUT NUCLEAR ATTACK AND COUNTER-ATTACK.

The final aspect of preliminary analysis is to discover vital issues which each side will argue. You will want to anticipate the most likely arguments of your opponent, so that you can answer those. Therefore, you spend time not only with your point of view, but also the opposing arguments. We shall once more use as our example the topic: "Resolved, that the United States and the Soviet Union should negotiate a mutually verifiable nuclear arms reduction treaty." In analyzing this topic, we might identify the following arguments, among many others.

ARGUING *FOR* THE PROPOSITION	ARGUING *AGAINST* THE PROPOSITION
I. There is a need for the superpowers to negotiate a mutually verifiable arms reduction treaty, because:	I. There is no need for the superpowers to negotiate a mutually verifiable arms reduction treaty, because:
A. The nuclear weapons stockpile has reached overkill proportions.	A. Technology (such as SDI or "starwars") will eventually render nuclear weapons useless.
B. The presence of so many weapons increases the likelihood of use.	B. It is our stockpile which deters aggression, for both nuclear and conventional warfare.
C. The effects of an all-out nuclear attack and counter-attack would be davastating	C. The U.S. is better equipped to survive a nuclear attack.
1. _____ of life could be obliterated.	D. The U.S. can only negotiate for peace effectively if we bargain from a position of strength.
2. The after effects of a nuclear exchange would destroy the world's ecological balance	
D. Tensions between the U.S. and the U.S.S.R. are on the increase.	

The arguments outlined above would lend themselves to many supporting arguments. Again, this does not begin to exhaust the possible areas. The more argument ideas you generate, the better prepared you will be to argue effectively.

Argumentative Support

In an argument, each side is obliged to *prove the case* presented. To prove a case means to provide argumentative support for a point of view or claim. Effective argumentative support comes from evidence and reasoning.

How do we know the things we know? When grease is on fire in the kitchen, if one tries to put out that fire with water, he/she will discover that water simply spreads out the fire; water does not extinguish a grease fire. On the other hand, baking soda provides the necessary chemical reaction. If you have been lucky enough to experience the grease fire phenomenon described above, you are fairly certain of the accuracy of these statements. Without direct experience (or to predict future events) people must rely on logical reasoning. Logical reasoning "is a process of seeing relationships, and then atempting to explain phenomena and predict future events. (Gossett, 1984, p. 67)." We are reasoning when we take objectively verifiable data and link them to probable truths which are not clearly identifiable. If I extinguish a grease fire with baking soda, I can predict that this will work each time based upon reasoning. We have thus created order out of an accident or state of disorder; or we have made things predictable through logic (Gossett, 1984).

Order out of disorder is created by supporting statements of claims through *proof*.

CLAIM OR STATEMENT

Evidence in support   **Reasoning in support**

Facts, examples, statistics, expert testimony   Induction, deduction, causal reasoning, analogy

As illustrated in this figure (above) proofs may come in the form of evidence or logic (reasoning). A unit of proof may be long and complicated or as brief as a sentence (Thompson, 1971): "We believe that F.A.A. Air Traffic Controllers fired because of the P.A.T.C.O. strike will not return to their jobs (claim) because of the consistent citations of law offered by President Reagan in defense of the firings (support by citing testimony of authority)."

Facts are citations of generally accepted truth. Facts are usually verifiable, the word fact is quite often abused. The rules that determine what consitutes a fact vary. The more academic rigor you can apply to determine the verity of your facts, the better your facts will be. Generally speaking, something you can observe with the senses, something recorded in history, something demonstrated by science, or a public statement constitute the soundest "facts" for argumentative support. Some facts qualify as facts depending upon your audience. There is, for example, a Flat Earth Society, which denies that our planet is a sphere. Often, there are facts which are directly contradictory. Right-to-life groups cite as fact that an abortion is much more dangerous to the health of the mother than carrying a child to term and giving birth. Pro-choice groups cite as fact that carrying a child to term and giving birth is much more dangerous to the mother's health than is an abortion.

Examples are instances which clarify, support, and dramatize as proof. Examples constitute effective proof if the following criteria are met:

- the examples are typical of what you want to prove
- the examples are significant in scope
- the examples are either common knowledge or come from reputable sources
- the examples are free of weaknesses such as atypicality, contradictory examples, lack of timliness, etc.
- the examples are persuasive by being dramatic, vivid, close to the listeners' experience, concise, etc.

Statistics quantify factual data (Ellis & Parro, 1970). Statistics provide hundreds or even thousands of examples in a single item of proof. Statistics make it possible to see the general picture, trends, and changes. They also draw comparisons (Thompson, 1971). The flip-side of statistics as proof is that stats very seldom actually *prove* anything; rather, they indicate probability. So, it is quite possible for statistics to be misleading Ellis & Parro, 1970). As a debater, you must be aware of what constitutes effective us of statistics so that you can apply high standards to *your* use of statistics, and so that you can see weaknesses in your *opponent's* use of statistics.

In effectively employing statistics, bear in mind that:

- the source should be verifiable and objective
- the source should be first hand if possible (not secondhand, such as census statistics *as reported* in the *National Enquirer*)
- statistical errors have not been committed in methodology (correct sample, adequate sample size, appropriate measures, statistically significant figures, meaningful averages) (Thompson, 1971).

One should also look for correct application of statistics to test their basis as proof. Statistics should be: possible to verify and offer a comparative base. There are statistics which are impossible to verify. An example might be: one out of every 200 Etruscans had two heads. Of course, this is a falsehood, but there's no way to sample a defunct civilization to test this statistic. The other factor, comparative base, is equally important. If we report that the Dallas Cowboys drew over half a million fans to their home games this year—is this a lot of people? Was attendance up from previous years? Don't let the opposition dazzle you with numbers. Demand that they "make sense" of the numbers by providing a comparative base for them.

Finally, we should be able to compare our comparative bases. If we say the United States Economy had a real growth rate of 1% in 1986, but the Belize economy had a real growth rate of 17%, can we conclude that Belize has a strong economic base? (Verderber, 1979).

The bottom line is use statistics, but use them with caution.

Expert testimony or the use of opinion is the final kind of evidence in support of a claim. This type of evidence would be any statement of opinion by someone who is in a position to know the facts; is an authority in his/her field; is relatively unbiased; is competent; is acceptable to the listeners; and is testifying in a way that expresses wisdom, pertinence, and clarity. Citing convicted murderer Ted Bundy's opinion on our criminal justice system is not as effective as citing Justice William Rhenquist's opinion, in terms of credible proof for most audiences. However, if Bundy were to espouse a view contrary to his self-interest, such as recommending that laws be passed to make capital punishment swift and immediate, then *he* might have greater credibility on this issue than Rhenquist.

Use of Evidence in Support

You should collect your evidence in a usable form. Many people use 4"x6" note cards. The card should contain pertinent data, the evidence itself, and a short summary of what the evidence demonstrates. An example is shown below:

Fires cause injury   *Washington Post*
and destroy property   1st June 1984
"Every year those fires result in more than 4000 injuries and
180 million dollars in property loss."

To utilize this evidence card in the context of your persuasive message, you would:

1. state your claim
2. present your evidence
3. tell why the evidence proves the point
4. summarize and move on to the next point.

The message for this point might sound like this:

Fire prevention is important because we can prevent injury and save property. The *Washington Post* reported that every year fires cause 4,000 injuries and result in 180 million dollars in property loss. In other words, if we could prevent these fires, there would be fewer injuries and we might save millions in property loss. This clearly points to the importance of preventing these household fires. Let's now take a look at how we might do just that. . . .

As another example of the use of evidence in support, let us examine a series of proofs. Let us suppose that you have discovered that scientific studies have revealed a way to coat cigarettes with a chemical treatment which causes the cigarette to extinguish itself when not puffed. These self-extinguishing cigarettes would protect the public from the many fires which are caused by smoldering cigarettes; and, in addition this self-extinguishing cigarette gives off less of the harmful substances in cigarette smoke, notably, tar, nicotine, and carbon monoxide. You have decided to claim the need for self extinguishing cigarettes on the basis of destructive fires and harms from noxious substances. You will also prove for your case that pressure from the tobacco industry on Congress has prevented this from coming about. Your message might include the following in making a case for self-extinguishing cigarettes: . . . what is disturbing about the fact that we don't have self-extinguishing cigarettes is the fact that people are dying in cigarette caused fires. *The Philadelphia Inquirer* reported that, "As many as 3,500 persons burn themselves to a crisp or suffocate from smoke inhalation in the U.S. every year in fires started by cigarettes. That figure has been well documented by the National Fire Protection Association. . . . It does not include the cigarette-caused fires listed as undetermined in origin (USE OF STATISTIC AS PROOF)." This quotation from a reputable newspaper clearly demonstrates that cigarettes left to smolder kill thousands, yet we do not have self-extinguishing cigarettes; furthermore, the self-extinguishing cigarette is safer for our bodies since the treatment reduces the emission of tar, nicotine, and carbon monoxide by 25%. The 25% reduction is documented by an H.E.W. study which linked serious diseases to tar and nicotene. Former H.E.W. secretary Joseph Califano said tar and nicotene were linked in the study to health problems, and "The study confirms that smoking can cause lung cancer . . . cancers of the mouth, esophagus, and bladder, and virtually every kind of heart disease (EXPERT TESTIMONY AS EVIDENCE). This study provides further reason for the production of self-extinguishing cigarettes: to reduce the incidence of chronic disease. Despite these compelling reasons, not one piece of legislation has been passed to require self-extinguishing cigarettes. Why? According to *The Washington Post* of June 1, 1980, "The tobacco industry always opposes any legislation which would control or regulate them, even if only to a small degree. They're a lot like the anti-gun control people. Even the littlest regulation they perceive as a move by the government to totally dominate them" (FACT PRESENTED AS EVIDENCE). So, the plain fact is there is a tobacco lobby which wants no regulation of the industry. I suppose it must be working. Because according to *The Congressional Record* dated June 4, 1980, "In the late 1920's the late Representative Edith Nourse introduced a bill to require cigarettes to be self-extinguishing. Although she introduced the bill in several successive sessions of Congress it was never passed" and "In 1975 the late Senator Phillip Hait introduced a bill which was passed by the Senate, but overwhelmingly defeated in the House." (EXAMPLES AS EVIDENCE) I think these examples of attempts to pass such legislation clearly show that Congress has not been willing to pass a law on self-extinguishing cigarettes. . . .

Use of Logical Reasoning in Support

It would be beneficial to you the reader if you received a very thorough treatment of logical reasoning, extensive in scope. Space does not permit that. However, some familiarity with logic will be required of good agrumentative speakers. Logical reasoning is a means of justifying claims through orderly and progressive thinking. In other words, you must *follow the rules* of a given kind of logic which you have chosen to use. Logical reasoning may require evidence, and it may not. We shall briefly examine the principles of logic types, and then look at a summary model which will work for all types of reasoning.

Deduction or deductive reasoning starts with an established GENERALIZATION and concludes about some SPECIFIC that falls under that generalization. We might readily apply deduction to our self-extinguishing cigarettes case. The generalization would be: "A law which protects consumers from hazards is a desirable law." From the preceding generality, we would reason to the specific case of self-extinguishing cigarettes in this way:

> A law which protects consumers from hazards is a desirable law. (Generalization)
>
> A law requiring self-extinguishing cigarettes protects consumers from cigarette-caused fires and noxious emissions. (Statement linking generalization to claim.)
>
> Therefore, a law which protects consumers by requiring self-extinguishing cigarettes is desirable. (claim)

Induction or inductive reasoning starts with a number of SPECIFIC INSTANCES and builds a GENERALIZATION. Inductive reasoning is employed in scientific research. In a way, induction was used in our self-extinguishing cigarettes case. The speaker cited several specific instances of attempts to pass a law requiring the production of self-extinguishing cigarettes. The conclusion or claim was that Congress is unwilling to pass such a law.

Causal reasoning establishes cause-effect relationships between a series of events. If event A preceded event B, did A cause B? Cause-effect relationships can only be determined to be probable. Absolute case would require that we examine every single case of A preceding B. We do, however, make educated guesses about cause based on whether the cause seems most likely or whether there might be another cause just as likely or more likely to produce the effect. If I conduct studies timing the smoldering of cigarettes, and determine that an unattended cigarette may burn for 20 minutes, and if I also discover that a cigarette smoldering for 10–15 minutes in upholstery or a mattress will ignite that mattress; I may then establish a causal link between ordinary cigarettes and fires. On the other hand, if one discovers that most heroin addicts at one time smoked marijuana, may that person logically conclude that smoking marijuana causes heroin addiction? Not on this evidence alone! It might also be that most heroin addicts were breast-fed as babies. Does breast feeding cause heroin addiction? Probable cause is an important aspect of proof in a policy debate. You will likely be looking at a problem and either predicting the effects of a proposed solution (cause) or examining a problem's effects and reasoning as to the probable cause.

Reasoning by analogy is most often simply an alternate form of causal or inductive reasoning. I have listed this form of reasoning as a separate category here because the employment of analogy can be a useful rhetorical tool. Analogies are comparisons. President Reagan reasoned by analogy during his 1980 presidential campaign against Jimmy Carter. Reagan explained in some of his mediated campaign rhetoric what he had done to increase government efficiency while he was governor of California. The analogy was made comparing state government to the Federal government. Reagan was arguing that if he saved California, a state which, were it a country, would have the fourth largest economy in the world, then wouldn't it follow that he could "bring America back," too.

Reasoning as Warranted Claim

The easiest way to synthesize the use of reasoning is to examine how arguments are constructed. A very useful tool devised by Stephen Toulmin is perhaps most utlitarian here in both constructing arguments and finding weaknesses in opponents arguments. In everyday discussions, we make claims as to things we believe. Sometimes we supply evidence to back our claims. The evidence we provide is the completion of an argument. If I say, "I know Rock Hudson was a homosexual because he died of Aids," then I am providing a bit of evidence and a claim, and contending that the evidence leads to the claim.

We will teach you the Toulmin model of reasoning by using the Rock Hudson case because it is a good way of understanding *how* most people reason. Understand that Toulmin was not concerned so much with how people *ought to* think, but rather, with how they *do* think. This is why we have chosen the Aids issue, because it is an emotional one, and therefore one by which we can demonstrate how people construct their arguments, right or wrong, logical or illogical.

Evidence _____ so _____ Claim
(Datum)

Rock Hudson   so   Rock Hudson was a
Died of Aids   homosexual
(Factual Statement)   (Inference drawn from Datum)

The assumption about Hudson's homosexuality is an *inference* or a conclusion indicated indirectly, as opposed to a verifiable piece of data or *datum* (such as Hudson died of Aids, medically verified).

Toulmin says that the argument is completed by a warrant, or connector between the inferred conclusion and the verifiable datum. Toulmin's basic model of an argument looks like the figure below.

Datum _____ so _____ Claim

since warrant

(Toulmin, 1958).

The warrant represents a relatively accepted generalization which has been arrived at. In our Hudson example, it might be this:

Datum _____ so _____ Claim
Rock Hudson   Rock Hudson was a
Died of AIDS   homosexual

Since
Warrant
Most Americans who contract
Aids have the disease
transmitted through homosexual
contact.

Warrants are not always stated. Quite often they are implied or assumed in ordinary conversation. In argumentation, one should *know* his/her warrants. The need to be aware of warrants is at the heart of sound bases for claims. Toulmin's basic model of an argument is not unlike diagramming a sentence to diagnose component parts. By diagramming an argument, one can begin to see where the weakness lies, and either build stronger arguments of one's own or see the weakness(es) in an opponent's arguments.

The basic model: *datum* so *claim,* since warrant is essentially complete. However, Toulmin built upon that basic structure to present an argument diagram which more thoroughly reflects a soundly stated argument. Toulmin added to the basic model a "qualifier" such as the word "presumably" or "probably." The qualifier was added since inferences are not absolutely true. In our Hudson example, we would structure as follows:

Datum ——————————— so ——————————— (qualifier) *Claim*
Rock Hudson   Presumably, Rock Hudson
died of AIDS   was a homosexual.

                 Since
                 Warrant

                 Most Americans who contract
                 AIDS have the disease transmitted
                 through homosexual contact.

Toulmin also added a "rebuttal" which serves to counter arguments for some other link between datum and claim. If we added a rebuttal to our Hudson argument, it might look like the diagram below:

Datum ——————————— so ——————————— (qualifier) *Claim*
Rock Hudson   Presumably, Rock Hudson was
died of AIDS   a homosexual

                                     unless
                                     Rebuttal
                                     Hudson contracted the disease
                                     through a blood transfusion
              since   or intravenous drug use.
              Warrant
              Most Americans who contract
              the disease have the disease
              transmitted through homosexual
              contact.

The final piece of the Toulmin puzzle is "backing." The backing provides support for the warrant. Warrants are established generalizations which may have been claims themselves in another argument. Backings support warrants much as datums lead to claims. Our completed diagram would be as follows:

DATUM _____ so _____ (Qualifier) CLAIM

    Since
    WARRANT   unless
                                 REBUTTAL

    which is true
    because of
    BACKING

Returning for the last time (thank heaven) to Rock Hudson, our argument would be completed thus:

DATUM _____ so _____ (Qualifier) CLAIM
Rock Hudson died   Presumably, Rock Hudson
of AIDS   was a homosexual.

    since   unless
    WARRANT   *REBUTTAL*
    Most Americans who contract the disease have   Hudson contracted the disease
    the disease transmitted through homosexual   ease through a blood trans-
    contact.   fusion or intavenous drug
                                         abuse.

    which is true because of

        BACKING
    Evidence gathered by the National Center for
    Disease Control on the spread of AIDS in this
    country.

Any argument will have these parts stated or inferred. As a debater, one should practice building and analyzing arguments based on the Toulmin model to be as thorough and logical as possible. Eventually, this will become an "instinctive" process in the analysis of argument. For now, you should work on remembering this basic structure of Toulmin's model and the purpose of each part.

Datum: factual evidence

Claim: conclusion drawn from datum

Warrant: connector generalization which justifies the link between datum and claim

Qualifier: a term to limit the absoluteness of an argument (rarely stated in competitive debate)

Rebuttal: response to counter arguments (also rarely stated in debate)

Backing: evidence in support of the warrant.

(c.f. Scheidel, 1967; Thompson, 1971; Gossett, 1984; Toulmin, 1958)

```
Datum _____ so _____ (Qualifier) Claim
              Since                    unless
              Warrant                  Rebuttal
              which is true
              because of
              Backing
```

MODIFYING AND CRITICIZING CLAIMS

The process of modifying and/or citicizing claims is called Refutation. We use refutation to show weaknesses in our opponent's arguments and rebuild our own. Refutation, then, is a sort of test of who has better arguments; and, ultimately, refutation offers decision makers grounds for discounting one side's arguments as opposed to the other side (Rieke & Sillars, 1984).

Refutation is a difficult process because you must learn to think and analyze quickly. In other words, you must hear the opponent's argument and determine the weakness so that you can refute that argument when it is your turn to speak. Of course, if you research and analyze your opponents' point of view as well as your own, you will have anticipated the opposing arguments, and will be better prepared to meet them (Verderber, 1979).

The basis for refutation depends upon the format for debate. In most debates, a speaker gets more than one opportunity to speak. So, then, if it were a matter of one speaker versus another, the first speaker would present his/her case and then the second speaker would present an opposing case, including refutation. The first speaker would then return to the speaker's platform for refutation. It might be that the second speaker would give a second refutation speech, and the first speaker a third. Such a pattern would be as follows.

1st speaker	6 minutes
2nd speaker	7 minutes
1st speaker	3 minutes
2nd speaker	4 minutes
1st speaker	2 minutes

Of course, any pattern would work which allows each side balanced opportunities to refute. You could just as easily face a situation where in there were four speakers for each side and the teams would have to refute for their partners:

1st speaker	pro side
1st speaker	con side
2nd speaker	pro side
2nd speaker	con side

By following such patterns as those above, each side of the proposition builds his/her own arguments (proves the case) and attacks the arguments of the opponent (refutes the opposing case).

If you faced an argumentative speaking situation wherein you alternated speeches, you would require a set of notes for refuting. Usually, this set of notes takes the form of a chart which aligns arguments in rows and refutational speeches in columns (see example below).

ARGUMENT CHART

My Arguments	My Opponent's Arguments	My Refutation	My Opponent's Refutation
(Argument 1)	(Refutation of Argument 1)	(Refutation of Refutation Argument 1)	(Refutation of Refutation of Refutation of Argument 1)
(Argument 2)	(Refutation of Argument 2)	(Refutation of Refutation of Argument 2)	ETC.
(Argument 3)			

(Adapted from Rieke & Sillars, 1984)

Take careful notes of the key points and also the proof offered. Put both the claim and proof on your chart. These notes will give you the best chance to effectively refute your opponent.

The Process of Refutation

Refutation involves four steps:

1. State the argument you will refute clearly.
2. Tell your listeners how you plan to refute so the listener can follow you.
3. Present your proof.
4. Summarize your refutation and tell why you have beaten the opponent's argument with the proof offered.

(Verderber, 1979; Thompson, 1971).

This process is repeated for each argument. An illustration may serve to clarify. Let us suppose that you are debating the proposition: "Resolved, that physical punishment for conduct problems in public school must be outlawed." Your opponent has put forth arguments on the risks a school district takes with corporal punishment. Your opponent has argued that the risks are too great because of lawsuits and physical harm to the disciplined child. Your response could be as follows:

1. My opponent has argued that we have to outlaw corporal punishment in the classroom because of risks.
2. My response to that argument will be that we have to have that option available for controlling conduct.

3. Dr. Charles Miller, Associate Professor of Education at Purdue Calumet, wrote in *Instructor,* March, 1980, "When the teacher, having exhausted other approaches, feels only physical punishment will prove corrective, then that choice should not be denied."

4. So, you see, we need to allow teachers the option of physical punishment. Otherwise, we prevent one possible corrective action for conduct problems. Of course we want to try other ways first, but teachers need this final option. So the risk argument is outweighed by the need for teachers to maintain order through every available means.

You may have already thought of counter-responses to the refutation above. That is the way argumentation works. As soon as one person presents an argument, a likely refutative response is also going to emerge for the other side.

Attacking the Proof

In order to criticize claims, a debater must find the weaknesses in the proof offerred by the opponent. There are weaknesses to look for in evidence, in reasoning, and one also needs to know about certain special kinds of logical fallacies.

Tests for evidence are usually those items which pertain to the accuracy and validity of the proof. For each type of evidence, certain criteria apply. If the debater used *facts* in support; the facts should be first hand reports, should evoke common agreement as to the truth of the fact, and there should be few if any contrary facts. In use of fact, it is also important to ask why a fact may be doubtful and whether a fact is actually an opinion or inference. If a debater used *examples* in support, one should examine the examples to see that those examples are typical, significant, and consistent with other kinds of proof offered. In addition, the example must be presented with omitting crucial details, come from a reliable source, and be more supportive of the claim than any negative examples possible which might contradict the claim. *Statistics* also have to meet certain criteria. We have already indicated some of these in our discussion of statistical proof, notably: reliable and first hand sources, use of appropriate statistical methodology, verifiability, and clear comparative base. It is also important to check the recency and possible bias of a statistic. *Expert opinion* as support also has to meet certain criteria. When using this form of proof, you may have weaknesses if: the opinion is not reasonable; the person is not an expert in a given area; the expert is biased, incompetent, or unaware of the impact of his/her opinion; if the quotation is out of context or quoted indirectly; or if the source of the expert opinion is unreliable (Thompson, 1971).

All these tests of evidence offer possible avenues of refutation. When your opponent presents some claim with evidence as proof, and you cast some doubt upon the proof, then you have refuted the claim.

Attacking the logic will call on your ability to do one of two things: either analyze the type of reasoning to find weaknesses or cast the argument in Toulmin's model to find weaknesses.

In arguing against *deduction,* one might argue against the generalization Or against the statement which links the generalization to the conclusion. As you may recall, our example for deduction was:

A law which protects consumers from hazards is a desirable law.

A law requiring self-extinguishing cigarettes protects consumers from cigarette-caused fires and noxious emissions.

Therefore, a law which protects consumers by requiring self-extinguishing cigarettes is desirable.

In attacking the generalization, one might well ask why laws are required to protect consumers. Is not the government that governs least the best. Is it not better to let the free market protect consumers? In attacking the statement linking the generalization to the claim, one might cast doubt on the significance behind the support offered for this statement. Are cigarette-caused fires not simply the result of carelessness? Doesn't the cigarette have to wind up smoldering on a bed or upholstery in order to start a fire? So what if we reduce noxious emissions by 25%? Isn't there still tar, nicotene, and carbon monoxide emitted? How much of these emissions are needed to constitute a health hazard?

In arguing against *induction,* one simply questions whether there are enough specifics to justify the claimed generalization. In our earlier example, we used induction, saying that there had been several attempts in the 1920's and one attempt in 1975 to pass legislation on self-extinguishing cigarettes. We generalized that Congress was unwilling to pass such a law. Do we have enough cases to conclude that Congress is unwilling? Why did the bills fail?

In arguing against *causal* reasoning, we try to show that a cause-effect relationship may not be correct. You can do this by:

1. Showing other causes more probable than the one cited.
2. Reporting circumstances that deny the cause-effect relationship.
3. Suggesting another cause which is more likely.
4. Identifying other effects.
5. Claiming there is absolutely no relationship between the opponent's probable cause and effect.

(Thompson, 1971).

We cited the example of the heroin-marijuana link above. We might also examine a popular causal argument in the case of the 1960 televised debates between John F. Kennedy and Richard Nixon. It was widely argued that since Kennedy looked better than Nixon (cause), Kennedy won the presidential race in 1960 (effect). However, Kennedy's idealism may have captured America's imagination during the "cold war," thus garnering votes Or the fact that many dead people "cast ballots" in Mayor Daley's Chicago may have turned the tide Or the fact that Kennedy was Catholic may have generated a block vote by Roman Catholics Or people may have remembered that Nixon was accused of taking illegal campaign contributions in previous elections. Any means of questioning causality weakens the strength of that logic.

Finally, in arguing against *analogy,* one can simply show how the comparison is invalid. Ronald Reagan claimed his effective programs as governor of California qualified him for the role of president. Is being governor the same as being president? Does the executive have more power in state government than at the Federal level? Are California's problems of the 1960's and 1970's the same as the nation's problems in the 1980's? Such questions cast doubt upon the analogy.

You may find it easier to utilize the Toulmin model of an argument. By casting an argument in Toulmin's form, you can quickly examine the *warrant* closely. The warrant is the usual location of argumentative weakness. One should also examine backings, rebuttals, and qualifiers if they are present, since these elements give other clues as to where weaknesses lie.

Specialized Fallacies

Finally, in attacking logic one may "be on the lookout" for logic fallacies. It is often the case that an argumentative message bases claims on what appears to be reasoning, but in fact is not logic at all (Gossett, 1984). Some of the most common logic fallacies are detailed below.

Partial or distorted facts are used in support of fallacious reasoning: "This is a nation founded by religious people, so we need a theocratic government where church and state are one." (Missing is the fact that these religious people fled from oppression by an official state church.)

Substitution of ridicule or humor for argument is common. In refutation, you can reduce an argument to absurdity but it must be done with sound reasoning; not a joke. An example of substitution of ridicule for argument might be: "Some people say that marriages would be better off with more openness in communication. So, I was open with my wife and told her she was a lousy cook and a lousy lover."

Assertion without proof is a common misuse of argumentation. Beware of such phrases as "Everybody knows that . . ." and "It is common knowledge that. . . ."

Appeals to sympathy are persuasive, but not logical. When a certain vice president was accused of illegal campaign contributions, his televised response was filled with such statements as "Pat doesn't have a fur coat. But, she does have a good respectable Republican cloth coat. And, I always tell her she looks good in anything." (Never were charges of illegal contributions specifically addressed!)

Appeals to prejudice and stereotype have become the norm in politics. For example, "what can you expect from a liberal like her?"

Appeals to tradition are again persuasive, but not logical. For example: "I know some of you ladies want to play in the marching band, but we have had an all male marching band since this school began."

Name calling or personal attacks often appear when logic is not seen as needed: "There goes that lunatic Khadafy duck shooting off his mouth again."

Begging the question means using emotion-laden language which assumes we all hold with the same belief: "Let's take a look at this idealistic bleeding-heart opposition to capital punishment. . . ."

"After this, therefore because of this" is an argument of questionable cause. Just because one event preceded another doesn't mean the first caused the second. For example: "I said he had a no-hitter going and the next pitch was a base hit, so I jinxed the pitcher."

Non sequitar (*it does not follow*) is really the absence of a warrant and/or datum for a claim: "Ferraro was not qualified for the vice presidency because she was a Congresswoman."

Arguing in a circle (circular argument) is a case of assumed proof: "Men should not be housekeepers because they are *men*."

Raising irrelevancies is a logic fallacy to distract attention from the immediate issue: "So why is privacy a Constitutional right? This whole argument reminds me of the battle for women's suffrage. . . ." (What about privacy and the Constitution?)

Substitution of prestige for argument may be persuasive, but the logic support is lacking: "I have listened to this undergraduate's conclusions regarding interpersonal persuasion, and they're fine for an uninitiated scholar. However, I have a Ph.D. in this area, and I disagree." (Specifically, what is wrong with the conclusions?)

The Slippery Slope fallacy assumes that if a little of something helps a lot then a lot of something will help that much more. Vitamin sales work on this fallacy. People assume that if "a little iron makes me feel peppy then four times the dosage will make me feel four times as peppy." The law of diminishing returns comes into play.

(Thompson, 1971).

127

Of course, there are other logic fallacies. However, you should learn to be wary of these in your own messages and the messages of others in examining the logic in a given point of view.

Remember that to refute, you should: plan for the opponent's arguments, take careful notes, refute (using the four basic steps), present a well organized set of responses, and provide sound proof.

SUMMARY

Argumentative speaking requires deep critical thinking and a great deal of background knowledge. Your preparation for debate speaking should include attention to each aspect of argumentation as listed below:

1. Analyze the topic.
   a. Provide a statement or proposition for debate focused upon an issue of policy, fact, or value.
   b. Begin preliminary analysis to discover: causes for debate, history and background, definitions, goals, and vital issues.
2. Know the bases for argumentation to advance and support claims.
   a. Seek evidence in support in the form of facts, examples, statistics, and expert opinion.
      (1) Create an evidence card file.
      (2) Use the four point formula for evidence as proof.
   b. Seek logical reasoning in support.
      (1) Build arguments based upon sound deduction, induction, causal reasoning, and reasoning by analogy.
      (2) Or examine your arguments as claims warranted from data (Toulmin's model).
3. Prepare for refutation so as to modify and criticize claims.
   a. Analyze your opponent's potential arguments.
   b. Know the basic requirements for refutation.
      (1) Prepare an argument chart for notes.
      (2) Follow the four step process to refute each argument.
      (3) Know the tests for evidence and reasoning.
      (4) Learn to recognize logic fallacies.

REFERENCES

Ellis, N. P. and Parro, P. (1970) *The debate experience.* Lafayette, Louisiana: Elco Press.
Gossett, J. S. (1984) Rational appeals in persuasive discourse. in H. T. Hurt & B. H. Spitzberg (eds & compilers) *Essays on human communication.* Lexington, Massachusetts: Ginn Custom Publishing.
Rieke, R. D. and Sillars, M. O. (1984) *Argumentation and the decision making process (2nd edition).* Glenview, Illinois: Scott, Foresman, and Company.
Scheidel, T. (1967) *Persuasive speaking.* Glenview: Scott, Foresman, and Company.
Thompson, W. N. (1971) *Modern argumentation and debate: principles and practices.* New York: Harper and Row Publishers.
Toulmin, S. (1958) *The uses of argument.* Cambridge: Cambridge University Press.
Verderber, R. F. (1979) *The challenge of effective public speaking* (4th ed.) Belmont, California: Wadsworth Publishing Company.

Free Speech and Persuasion

by Ron Manuto

12

Whoever would overthrow the liberty of
a nation must begin by subduing the
freeness of speech. —Cato

One might reasonably ask precisely what the function of speech is in human life. Most of us communicate not simply to relieve ourselves of emotion or opinion, though given the relative quality of some speech it makes one wonder. The primary purpose of speech is to induce cooperation. It is the medium by which our varying perspectives can be coordinated so that common goals can be achieved. Those of us in the discipline of communication realize that this is no small matter. So much of what we do when communicating clouds our capacity to comprehend, let alone reason. In an often quoted phrase, Isocrates understood better than most today the vital social function speech serves.

> For in the other powers which we possess, we are in no respect superior to other living creatures; nay, we are inferior to many in swiftness and in strength and in other resources; but, because there has been implanted in us the power to persuade each other and to make clear to each other whatever we desire, not only have we escaped the life of wild beasts, but we have come together and founded cities and made laws and invented arts; and, generally speaking, there is no institution devised by man which the power of speech has not helped us to establish. (Isocrates, 354 B.C., p. 26)

Speech enables us to develop as an individual within a social community. Amid the varied responses of others, the individual becomes capable of organizing and integrating information into patterns of behavior and stability. What is critical in understanding the importance of speech is that what was once perhaps no more than a gesture becomes a significant symbol. When the individual learns to call out a word, and the word affects others in the same way, the stage of genuine language is reached. It is through the social process that we transcend our biology acquiring a sense of self and a mind. This somewhat impulsive animal called homo sapien becomes human and has acquired the potential to reason. (Meade, 1934)

The cycle of birth, life and death is neither inherently good or bad. The laws which govern nature operate independently of our relative ability to know and understand them; they exist and function in spite of our efforts to manipulate them. Yet, because of the social acquisition of speech, we have this capacity to inquire and reason about life, to seek an understanding of the irrational, the unexplainable, the mystifying. Behind such inquiry is purpose. It is speech which has allowed for such purpose, for a quality of mind. Hence, to *freely speak* in order to contact others, to co-operate in the achievement of common ends, is indispensible to personal and collective survival. To suppress or strictly regulate the human effort to communicate with his/her own kind is to distort and possibly control the fragile process of individual and collective development.

Thomas Jefferson argued for freedom of speech because he believed that reason and free inquiry were the only effective agents against error. No one person is infallible, including Supreme Court judges. Neither are all people necessarily driven by a concern for the well-being of others. Adolph Hitler and Joseph Stalin were so possessed by their fanatical visions of world order that they were willing to sacrifice the lives of millions of people as the means to their political ends. The Reverend Jim Jones became so obsessed with his vision of a new socialist society, that he was willing and apparently successful in coercing over 900 people into committing suicide. History is filled with the distressing stories of charismatic leaders who were willing to sacrifice the lives of others, to view them as instruments, objects of economic and political policy. What is perhaps most troubling is the extent, via no more than the expression of ideas and emotions, of their success. Difference in perspective, an orientation to the reality of living, should be an understandable phase of growth. One cannot fully expect to know what the other is thinking or feeling without some context of dialogue or conversation. However, once the difference in experience is articulated, the human animal may often revert to some primal state of defence and aggression rather than the more stabling force of reason. We are conditioned to fear conflict, and more troubling, to resolve it destructively rather than rationally. Yet, conflict in one form or another is a natural part of most people's social and political experience. The critical question of survival is always the manner in which conflict is to be resolved. If the resolution is to be peaceful as well as fair, then one has to be capable of reason. It is this view of human nature, the individual as a choice-making, reasoning creature, that the First Amendment to the U.S. Constitution reflects. In respecting and believing in the essential virtue rather than vices of human nature, the framers of the First Amendment placed severe restrictions on government from interfering with the experience of its citizens. So the admonition:

> Congress shall make no law respecting an establishment of religion, or prohibiting the free exercise thereof; or abridging the freedom of speech, or of the press; or the right of the people to peaceably assemble, and to petition the Government for a redress of grievances.

At first notice, these restrictions appear explicit. Yet, somehow the notion has persisted that "offensive" or "harmful" ideas could, should, and would be punished. Further, the amendment says nothing about what the individual state legislatures might do or not do. But in 1927, Section One of the 14th Amendment (the due process clause) was incorporated in the First Amendment by the Supreme Court in *Fiske v. Kansas* and what was denied to the Congress was then denied to the states. While this seemed to be a breakthrough for First Amendment freedoms by creating more consistent national standards, the question of what kind of communication deserves protection is still not completely answered. Upon his retirement, the late Supreme Court Justice William O. Douglass claimed:

> . . . the First Amendment states that Congress shall make no law abridging the freedom of speech. The word does not seem ambiguous, though many judges read the words Congress shall make no law to mean Congress may make some laws. (Douglas, 1976, p. 20)

As a result, the conflict between your right to say, print or picture as measured against the community's right to restrict and/or punish in order to protect the general welfare or maintain the requirements of public order is in a constant process of change and refinement. According to some observers, the Supreme Court has failed to establish a unifying theory of the free speech clause, nor has it reached a consensus of premises or values upon which first amendment cases could be decided. (BeVier, 1978) If accurate, this is an important criticism because without some form of a unified theory of free expression our right to persuade, inform or entertain can be corrupted on the basis of ad hoc judicial decisions.

THE VALUES OF FREE SPEECH

In societies where more rather than less free expression exists, one might ask just what values are embedded in its exercise? One of the outstanding contributors to the theory of free expression is Thomas I. Emerson. In his book, *Toward a General Theory of the First Amendment* (1966), Emerson argues that free expression is indispensible to the achievement of four values. They are: 1) individual self-fulfillment, 2) the attainment of truth, 3) participation in the decision-making process, and 4) the balance between stability and change.

As noted earlier, self and mind are socially produced. The capacity of any one person to develop will be a function of his/her capacity to freely associate and interact. In more totalitarian societies, this right can be highly restricted. Even if we are allowed to associate, for example in the context of education, if there are limits on the kinds of ideas we may examine, discuss or advocate, then human development can become arrested rather than extended. This value of self-fulfillment essentially reflects a faith in students, educators, as well as citizens, in their ability to handle even the most "dangerous" of ideas or images. Accuracy in Academia is an example of an organization that does not have that faith; they feel that higher education is staffed by left-wing idealogues who are attempting to indoctrinate rather than instruct. Yet, most students realize that it is nearly impossible to have lived through four years of college instruction and not be exposed to an incredible variety of thought and perspective.

Emerson's second concern, the attainment of truth, is not only a value contained in the First Amendment but in the entire sphere of culture. The ancient Greeks were the first to discover that the survival of the republic would be a function of intense public deliberation by the widest variety of people and perspectives. To one famous Greek thinker, Plato, this was a dangerous precept. He did not conceal his lack of faith in most men's (women were not even an issue in those years) ability to attain the truth; in fact all the dialogues represent a focused attack on those teaching the powers of persuasion. Only a chosen few, highly trained in dialectics, should seek the truth. Plato would undoubtedly be appalled by the concept of a modern university educating thousands of students, as well as the entire concept of representative government. Knowledge and truth are believed by others such as Emerson to best be attained by the fullest discussion. In this context ideas as well as policies will stand or fall when tested in the marketplace. And again, this premise assumes a kind of faith that people seek the "best" judgment and that they will be rigorous and individually responsible in its attainment. There are always high stakes when one seeks to persuade, for when not done well the outcomes can be disastrous. Contemporary history is littered with examples of policies not rigorously examined; when implemented the results were often tragic. The internment of Japanese-Americans during World War II is one such example.

Participation in the decision-making process should be a rather obvious value in a democracy. But in order to do so there must be the will and the fullest possible disclosure of information. Secrecy in government, an affliction of the modern state, severely restricts the quality of discussion and the attendant decisions. Disinformation campaigns designed to achieve military or political objectives often mislead our own representatives, as well as the checking power of the press. Another important component of this value is readiness and ability. Low voter turn out statistics reflect an unwillingness of many thousands to exercise their rights. Participation in the life of the nation should be an unquestioned responsibility. However, it is also the case that people should be prepared to do so. According to Alexander Meiklejohn, one of the most influential first amendment theorists, government has the primary responsibility to educate its people so they will have the wisdom and dignity of governing citizens. He argues strongly that the issue of educational preparation of citizenship precedes any discussion of free speech, for how can it be achieved if people are not able?

In an age of intense social and political change, all communities are precariously balanced at the edge of civil turmoil. There has been and continues to be a bewildering array of movements and issues confronting us. The mind reels in the attempt to comprehend it all, from ethnic groups to gay rights, from workers to prison inmates; all have petitioned for a redress of grievance. If order is a requirement of social life, then a central question is always how to preserve order in the face of dissent. Emerson believes that the balance between stability and change can best be achieved by the fullest freedom of expression; it allows for the release and articulation of ideas so that their validity may be measured and acted upon. Suppression of dissent seems to always be present in those who are in control, that dark tendency in most of us to resist or deny what is different or requires change. While suppression, whether intellectual or physical, may work in the short term, the problem really never goes away. Even the Soviets have painfully learned that threatening dissidents with exile to the Gulag does not remove the intense displeasure with policy. Rather, suppression only enhances the courage to criticize.

It is not difficult to understand how closely guarded these four values are to those with a sense of history and commitment to the human capacity for reason. In education, government and the law, these values are appealed to incessantly. Our concern with authoritarian organizations at home or abroad usually is based on a violation of or more one of these values and they often become the rallying cry for change.

The difficulty with the achievement of these values in relation to First Amendment freedoms is that our own history reveals some rather dramatic discrepancies between their existence ideally (what should be) and social or political realities (what has been/is). The following is a classic example from the recent past where the government attempted, with temporary success, to control and crush dissent.

THE ESPIONAGE ACT, 1917

As suggested earlier, a critical assumption underlying the First Amendment is that human beings are essentially rational creatures. In order to exercise this capacity to reason, and, most importantly, to govern themselves, the state must be restrained from interfering with speech and press, with assembly and association. A free and open market-place of ideas is held to be the necessary prerequisite to democratic decision making.

Yet, in periods of dramatic change, unrest, or war, the voice of reason is often the first victim and we appear to revert to some ancient campfire where fear and suspicion rule our nature. Prior to World War I, the nation was deeply divided, not only over the issue of war and peace, but a whole host of social, economic and political controversies. Once at war, a kind of madness took hold of our affairs, and the level of intolerance and hatred from what we claimed we despised in our enemies, suddenly became a common part of our domestic behavior. The passage of the Espionage Act in 1917 (and as amended on 1918, the Sedition Act), and its subsequent enforcement through 1921, represents the first, most vivid, and widespread examples of state sanctioned suppression in our nation's history.

While the war with Germany was the essential catalyst for this unparalleled wave of repression, the events which shaped this First Amendment crisis were complex and reveal divisions in belief and value present at the nation's birth. The struggle for reform, a more equitable society, has always been a driving force in our history. For some fifty years before World War I, the activities of the reform movement intensified around specific issues. There had been the Greenback Movement, the Grange, the Farmer's Alliances, the Populists, the Free Silverites, the Progressives, and Woodrow Wilson and the New Freedom. In each case, there was a call for greater governmental control over the "abuses" by the upper economic and propertied classes. The nation's involvement in international affairs was a natural outgrowth of its increasing economic development, and as the war in Europe came closer, the class war quickened over U.S. domestic and foreign policy. The reformers tended largely to be isolationists while the conservative capitalists were more likely to favor intervention. More importantly, the war provided the necessary political cover to move against the moderate and radical elements of the reform movement.

> Whether accidentally or as a result of cold calculation, it is a fact that almost immediately after the beginning of WWI, people of the political right used the war as an excuse to attack people of the left. They did so by accusing leftists of being disloyal . . . because the leftists would not change their views (critical of the capitalist system), the rightists were given an unparalleled opportunity to attack and crush them. (Peterson & Fite, 1957, p. 45)

The instrument of that attack was the Espionage Act of 1917.

PRESIDENT WILSON AND DISSENT

Though he instituted nearly all of the proposals of the Progressive movement, Woodrow Wilson was hardly a radical reformer. Like Theodore Roosevelt, he was not inherently against the trusts and monopolies, but he was politically sensitive to the danger of their abuses. In terms of foreign policy, he initially insisted on American neutrality and was angered by any discussion of military preparedness or planning. However, once he concluded that war with Germany was inevitable, he found in conservatives the needed political support. With the increased possibility for war, federal authority for the first time in our history would be used to unify the people and curb if not break the back of any dissent. "I'm in a hurry," he said at a meeting of the Daughters of the American Revolution, "to have a line-up, and let the men who are thinking first of other countries stand on one side, and all those that are for America first, last, and all the time, on the other side." (Baker & Dodd, 1962, p. 377)

In his third state of the nation speech to Congress, he claimed there was a need for legislation to deal with "disloyal" activities. This was a direct reference with what were then called hyphenates, i.e., the foreign born. In 1917, there were fifteen million immigrants in the United States and their loyalty was questioned more out of a xenophobic streak rather than any significant lack of patriotism. Particularly suspect were the Irish and German-Americans.

Because of pervasive isolationist feelings in the country, Wilson carefully began to consider ways to suppress any dissent. It was a shrewd move; he could play on the concerns many Americans had about radical activity in general and immigrants in particular. Newspapers for years had been running stinging articles on socialist organizations, particularly the International Workers of the World, characterizing the latter as the most serious menace the present system of society has ever been called upon to face. Whether or not Wilson's actions were politically motivated or merely that these groups were personally distasteful is difficult to ascertain, but when war came, he went at them with a vengeance:

> The President was a man who could tolerate little criticism of himself or his policies at any time. Anticipating the necessity of coercing total national unity if a national emergency occurred, he began eliminating criticism by screening out people he was convinced the majority of Americans would feel had no business expressing strong, controversial views on the proper course of the nation. . . . The care with which the administration had moved toward criminalizing dissident expression created a precedent which, once war was declared, could be used to transfer the same stigma borne by aliens to other groups whose support for the war had not been 100 percent from the beginning. (Murphy, 1979, p. 56)

From the country's earliest political battles, the power of the national government has been a source of concern in regard to individual liberties, and outside of the short-lived Alien and Sedition Act of 1798, there had been little in the way of formally monitoring or controlling public expression. In a major reversal, nearly all the resources of the national government embarked on a systematic effort to mold the opinion of its citizens; it deliberately moved to suppress individualism and diversity of thought, and thereby, laid the foundations for a surveillance state.

PASSAGE AND ENFORCEMENT

When President Wilson asked Congress for a declaration of war on April 2, 1917 he included in his statement the claim of widespread spying and criminal intrigue by German agents. While Germany did make a concerted effort to propagandize their position and cause turmoil, they were largely ineffective, even among the strongly anti-British Irish-American. Yet, as early as December 1915, the President began his disloyalty theme:

> I'm sorry to say that the gravest threats against our national peace and safety have been uttered within our own borders. There are citizens of the United States, I blush to admit, born under other flags . . . who have poured the poison of disloyalty into the very arteries of our national life. (Ellis, 1975, p. 190)

On June 15, 1917, after nine weeks of hearings and debates as well as seventeen revisions, the Espionage Act became law. It would punish false statements or reports intended to "interfere with the operation or success of the military or naval forces" and any attempt to "cause insubordination, disloyalty, mutiny or refusal of duty in the military or naval forces." Title XII empowered the Post Office to make "non-mailable any matter violating the act or advocating treason, insurrection, or forcible resistance to any law of the United States." (Chafee, 1941, p. 102)

Critics attempted to sound the alarm that the act represented a clear violation of the First Amendment, but the nation was in a patriotic fever. In testimony before the House Judiciary Committee, notable socialist, pacifists and suffragettes such as Norman Thomas, Ida Waters, Jane

Addams and John Reed, attempted to point out that the law was vague and gave the administration, not the courts, the power to stifle criticism. The committee chairman, Congressman Edwin Webb, North Carolina, argued that "Criticism could cause dissension" and people would simply have to postpone discussion until the war was over.

Reed argued that the Congress was adopting "Prussianism to defeat it" and that regulation of this kind would destroy democratic institutions. The committee insisted that the act would in no way curtail valid criticism; its intent was to deal with spies. Senators Robert M. LaFollette, George Norris and James Vardaman attempted to speak out but they were already being bitterly denounced in and out of Congress for not supporting the war. Two days before the act's passage, Senator William Borah eloquently and prophetically lashed out against the growing restraint of public discussion:

> Then followed, naturally, the proposition that in time of war we have no Constitution; that everything rests in the discretion of the Executive and Congress. When the question was asked how could people be denied the right to express their opinion when the Constitution is clear and unmistakable in its terms, the only reply that could be made, that during the war the guarantees in this fundamental law relative to liberty of speech and of private rights were in some way or other suspended . . . it is a doctrine fraught with evils the consequences of which no man can foresee or tell. (Brown, 1977, pp. 14–15)

Once the war was declared, the President became obsessed with the potential disloyalty of certain segments of American society, including the press. Besides pushing for the Espionage Act, he instituted a series of other measures to tighten his grip on any criticism of government policy:

April 6, 1917:	President issued regulations for conduct and control of "enemy" aliens forbidding them to publish any attack against the government
April 7, 1917:	Issued a secret executive order authorizing removal of any federal employee thought by superiors to be a loyalty risk (there were several thousand investigations through 1918).
April 14, 1917:	Created Committee on Public Information (CPI).
April 28, 1917:	Issued executive order extending censorship authority to Navy of all messages sent over cable and land telegraph lines, including all American news reports sent to foreign countries.
October, 1917:	Congress empowered the President control over all international communication and through the Post Office, absolute censorship over foreign language press, who were to provide the Postmaster General with literal translations for approval.
October, 1917:	President establishes Board of Censorship by executive order. The Board is empowered to examine any and all communication, including private letters of anti-interventionists and radicals. (Murphy, 1979, pp. 74–75)

The last measure, justified as a response to growing mob violence, was the May 16, 1918 amended version of the Espionage Act (called the Sedition Act). Passed at the request of Attorney General Thomas Gregory, the bill added nine more offenses broad enough to encompass even the slightest disagreement with anything "American." It is considered by legal scholars to be one of the most repressive and unnecessary pieces of legislation ever passed by a United States Congress.

The sudden loss of constitutional memory was deepened by a growing sense of fear, hostility and state-sanctioned repression. As if federal control of the content and character of discussion was not enough, over one-third of the state legislatures passed bills further restricting speech and assembly (criminal synidicalism laws). These laws were used to crush the radical spectrum of the labor movement as well as other organizations criticizing capitalism and/or the war. Signs of a national hysteria were everywhere:

> During the spring of 1918, news stories from all sections of the country told of people being beaten by mobs of superpatriots. Sometimes, it was for not displaying the flag, for objecting to the draft law, for criticizing American soldiers of the associated powers; but whatever the cause, the safest policy for one's physical well-being in many communities was to remain silent. (Peterson & Fite, 1957, p. 215)

The national government, primarily through the CPI, was carefully cultivating such attitudes. Hand-in-hand with these extensive propaganda efforts, came the nearly total suppression of dissent.

Besides President Wilson, the two principal agents in the administration enforcing the terms of the Espionage Act were Attorney General Thomas Gregory and Postmaster General Albert Burleson. Gregory had a force of more than three hundred agents under his command (forerunner to the FBI) to investigate the war-related activities of aliens and citizens. He encouraged the nation's local police chiefs to keep their eyes on "known" pacifists and German sympathizers. When he encouraged every American to report their suspicions about their neighbors to the Department of Justice, his office was flooded with thousands of accusations. Federal agents were also used in the persecution of the International Workers of the World. Under Gregory's tenure, over two thousand cases were prosecuted under the Act and 877 were convicted and sentenced.

Combined with state syndicalism laws, as well as city ordinances, from 1917 to 1921, thousands of individuals found themselves faced with criminal prosecution for advocating unpopular ideas. The administration of justice had gone mad. Never before or since had so many Americans experienced so powerful an effort of government control over the political system. Further, it is difficult to know how many others of conscience were restrained from speaking out for fear of prosecution; but these trials, as with all political trials, became powerful symbols of admonition to anyone concerned or confused about governmental intent.

Postmaster General Burleson was equally ambitious in exercising censorship powers. "Anti-war" material could be excluded from the mails without a court order; he could do this merely "upon evidence satisfactory to him." (Peterson & Fite, 1957) Although Wilson told the country's newspaper editors that Title XII would not be used to suspend civil liberties, Burleson did just that. In a secret memorandum to local postmasters, he directed them to:

> Keep a close watch on unsealed matters, newspapers, etc., containing matter which is calculated to interfere with the success of any disloyalty, mutiny or refusal of duty in the military . . . or otherwise embarrass or hamper the government in conducting the war. (Murphy, 1979, p. 110)

Within a month after passage of the Espionage Act, fifteen publications were excluded from the mails. One of the most celebrated instances involved the *Nation,* which published an article in September 1918, entitle, "Civil Liberty Dead." The editorial denounced the affair as "official anarchy," and suggested the President re-examine his "liberalism" and inquire into "what is being done to make democracy unsafe in America". The publication was held up for four days until the President personally intervened even though he continued to publicly support Burleson, who went on to further deny "second-class mailing privileges to twenty-two socialist newspapers and a wide range of pamphlets, including one by the National Civil Liberties Bureau which deplored mob violence." (*Nation,* 1918) Sadly, Burleson's arbitrary and repressive actions throughout the war were ultimately upheld by the Supreme Court.

Why the general public tolerated such a systematic suspension of the Bill of Rights is difficult to understand today. Outside of a handful of persistent critics, who were effectively neutralized or silenced with jail sentences, there was little reaction or consideration of the immediate and long-term effects of a steady expansion of the government's repressive mechanisms and policies. Perhaps, it was the war and the effect of the well-organized propaganda campaign by the CPI that prevented public concern. Or perhaps it was in the difficulty of viewing the Wilson adminstration, which instituted major domestic reforms, as doing anything questionable. There was a lack of awareness of the importance of civil liberties; it had no hold on people's imaginations and to criticize the government in this time frame took inestimable courage.

THE SUPREME COURT

Prior to 1919, the scope of the First Amendment had never been tested. Exactly what was allowed in the way of expression and under what circumstances was unknown. There was no case law from the Supreme Court, no guidelines for the lower courts in the face of legislative invasion. With the passage of the Espionage Act, the court received its chance. The initial test of the Act's constitutionality came in *Schenck v. United States* (1919). Schenck was General Secretary of the Socialist party, and along with several other party members, had mailed leaflets to draft-age men urging defiance of conscription. The government found the leaflet in violation of Title I, Section 3 of the Espionage Act and subsequently indicted and convicted Schenck, et. al. This case is significant for several reasons. First of all, it is the seminal work in First Amendment law. Secondly, it tragically upheld the constitutionality of the Espionage Act, which paved the way for other convictions, including Eugene Debs. Thirdly, it is important because in writing the opinion for the majority, Justice Oliver Wendell Holmes sets forth the clear and present danger doctrine, which is the court's first effort to reconcile the conflicting claims of national security and freedom of expression. Holmes justification for conviction ran as follows:

> We admit that in many places and in ordinary times the defendants in saying all that was said in the circular would have been within their constitutional rights. But the character of every act depends upon the circumstances in which it is done. The most stringent protection of free speech would not protect a man in falsely shouting fire in a theatre causing a panic. it does not even protect a man from any injunction against uttering words that may have the effect of force. The question in every case is whether the words are used in such circumstances are of such a nature as to create a clear and present danger that they will bring about the substantive evils that Congress has a right to prevent. (Holmes, 1919, p. 52)

Holmes' opinion raised issues that are still a matter of controversy. The First Amendment appears explicit, i.e., Congress shall make no law . . . yet, Holmes provides a qualification which in effect says that in certain circumstances (war, crisis) Congress can make some laws. He employs as a justification the hypothetical analogy of a man falsely shouting fire in a theatre. Granted, as a general proposition in specialized circumstances, the right of expression cannot be considered absolute. In the Schenck case, however, there was a fundamental difference in the circumstances being compared. While Schenck may have "wrongly" advocated resistance to national policy, he did not "falsely" do so. The relative validity of his speech (the content of the leaflet) was not an issue, merely the political climate of war.

There is little question that Schenck attempted to obstruct the draft. He admitted doing so. However, that merely begs the question of individual responsibility. Nowhere did Schenck physically act to block the draft; he merely advocated others not participate if called. Holmes' paradigm is clear: if the words (valid or invalid) lead to a "substantive evil," speech is not protected. Yet, the words in this case were not examined. Further, embedded in such an analysis is the view of human nature contrary to that in the First Amendment. It assumes an irrational response; somehow by the mere fact of reading Schenck's leaflet, prospective inductees will collapse in their ability to rationally choose. Holmes' opinion sanctions suppression of thought and expression that Congress thinks *may* lead to "harm," though the state assumes no burden of proof that the words in each case did in fact do so. The focus became circumstance and not words, and the right to redress grievance in a time of crisis was seriously eroded.

The years 1917–1921 were not admirable ones in our history. Panic, violence, and repression were commonplace. The Bill of Rights was essentially suspended for those who resisted state or federal policies. There was a disquieting acquiesence over the organized and systematic abuse of civil liberties by the three branches of government, an acquiesence in times of felt crisis which still lingers. The Supreme Court, the court of last resort responsible for protecting and creating a climate or reason and discussion, discovered a rationale which politically sanctioned fear and conspiracy. The period created a paradigm of repression. Those who later challenged established authority were to see it again.

LIMITS OF FREE SPEECH

Hardly any constitutional scholar, social critic, or educator believes that free speech is an absolute right in all cases. Some restraints on free expression should be apparent, particularly when it conflicts with other, equally legitimate rights of individuals or of the state. Even Alexander Meiklejohn, one of the free speech theorists who comes closest to maintaining an absolutist position, argues that the First Amendment was obviously not designed to give immunity from every use of speech. The central question is always where and on what grounds can we justifiably draw the line.

Meiklejohn suggests that in the interest of self-government, which is the controlling value upon which the First Amendment rests, there should be *no* limits. Freedom to educate, to consider the achievements of philosophy and the sciences, literature and the arts, as well as the freedom to discuss all issues related to self-government, must occur in an unrestrained atmosphere. We, the people, should have the sovereign power over these activities, not the institutions or agents of government. (Meiklejohn, p. 257)

However, Meiklejohn does draw some lines. The word "peaceable" is important. Government may regulate the time, place and manner in which expression occurs so as to protect the requirements of public order. This is the positive, supportive role government must play. Without order, and a fair procedure for all to contribute to the discussion, the exercise of speech can be obstructed. What cannot be limited, regulated or controlled is the *content* of speech. In addition, there are some forms of communication which are not directly related to self-government, and therefore, may have less value and not deserve the full protection of the First Amendment. Libel, slander, obscenity, false advertising, and communication related to the commission of crimes are all forms of speech which never have been given First Amendment protection by the courts. One can easily see how these forms of speech, with the possible exception of obscenity, may lead to demonstrable harms.

The problems with obscenity are incredibly complex. In 1957, the Supreme Court ruled that obscenity was a form of speech not deserving of First Amendment protection. The consistent difficulty has been in defining precisely what obscenity is. Further, the argument that obscene words or images have no social redeeming value goes begging. Even if, as many feminists claim, the characterizations of women in erotica and pornography is dehumanizing, the proposed solution of censorship is disquieting. There may be less drastic means available. Racist speech is a comparable example. Is the solutions to suppress or employ it as an educational tool? We should constantly remind ourselves via the marketplace of ideas rather than the censor's blue pen that there are those among us who not only have a distorted opinion of women, but of human beings generally. Evil or harmful thoughts will not go away simply because we punish people for expressing them. In addition, the implication of the censor's position is that most people do not have the capacity to make judgments and thereby need protection from themselves. This patronizing view of people is in itself as degrading as those who conceive women as instruments of male power or pleasure.

Even if this cynical perception of people is correct, how can a word or image be responsible for human action? Over time it may be a contributing fact in shaping attitudes, but it is the individual's responsibility for the behavior which results. Not all who see dramatized acts of aggression go out and attack the first person they see; neither do all who have at one time or another seen "hard-core" pornography desire to commit sado-masochistic acts against women. Some are actually saddened that any person would need such images to be sexually stimulated.

BASIC LEGAL DOCTRINES OF FREE SPEECH

To the average person, the law can be a confusing, unsettling field of experience. Completely understanding the meaning of legal decisions is not unlike visiting China for the first time; everything is strange and new, elusive, yet intriguing. But finally what one must come to know is that the activity of legal decision-making is composed of people and the rewards of fighting one's way through the intricacies of legal culture can be as rewarding as traveling to China and coming to understand a people one did not know before. Those who have sat on the Supreme Court since 1919, when the first major doctrine of free speech was articulated, are generally the same as anyone of us. They bring to their task somewhat the same beliefs, values and attitudes shared by the rest of us. The one essential difference is that they have the responsibility and authority to draw lines to what is allowed and why and what is not. Reading the cases in historical sequence is like reading a great political novel. The crises of war and civil unrest, intolerance and fear, courage and genius, find their way into that austere building in the same way they do into our classrooms and homes. While exciting, their task is not enviable. Over the years, several doctrines or tests of free speech have been developed and refined. The following is a brief description of some of the more important ones.

1. *Clear and Present Danger Test.* As cited earlier, this test of political speech was developed by Chief Justice Oliver Wendell Holmes in the *Schenck* case. He argued that there were unique circumstances in which speech could legitimately be suppressed. In later cases, Holmes and Justice Louis Brandeis modified the preferred position given the legislature by stating that the danger in question had to be immediate before the government could suppress. In *Whitney v. California* (1928), Brandeis emphasized that "no danger flowing from speech can be deemed clear and present, unless the incidence of the evil apprehended is so imminent that it may befall before there is an

139

opportunity for full discussion" (Brandeis, 1927, p. 374). The idea of imminence was eventually incorporated into the law in the 1967 case *Brandenburg v. Ohio* (1968). Now an individual cannot be prosecuted for the content of his/her speech unless the government can prove that the language in question is in fact a direct incitement and unless it can also be proven that the language in question will in fact produce such lawless action. Under such conditions, it is currently quite difficult for the state to secure a prosecution on the basis of advocacy, however reprehensible it may be.

2. *Prior Restraint Test.* The prohibition against the state suppressing or censoring the expression of ideas before the fact is rooted in the historical experience of England's licensing laws. This is not to say that one cannot be held responsible for what he/she prints or speaks, merely that to restrain prior to publication is to destroy the freedom. English licensing laws were terminated in 1695, but it was not until 1931 that the U.S. Supreme Court ruled on the issue in *Near v. Minnesota* (1931). Here, the court held that a Minnesota law which allowed for an injunction against the expression of "malicious" or "scandalous" information as a public nuisance was unconstitutional. The court did however point out that there were some unusual circumstances in which the state could suppress, e.g., interference with a war effort, enforcement of laws against obscenity, and to prevent violence or the violent overthrow of the nation. Even though such "exceptional" circumstances were not fully explained in the case, the government does have a heavy burden of justification whenever it attempts to suppress before the fact. One of the extraordinary applications of this doctrine was in *The Pentagon Papers* case, where the Nixon Whitehouse attempted to block publication by *The Washington Post* and the *New York Times* of "classified" documents related to our activities in Vietnam on national security grounds. The case is worthy of examination by all students of free speech and persuasion for it highlights the tension between the natural tendency of elected officials to conceal errors of judgement of one hand and the people's right to know on the other. In this case, the court quickly ruled that the government failed to meet its burden and the subsequent publication of the papers had a tremendous impact upon the national debate over the war.

3. *Balancing Test.* This test was developed when two competing constitutional issues were in question. For example, in an effort to prevent publicity affecting a free trial for an accused, a Nebraska judge imposed a gag rule on the press (*Nebraska Press Association v. Stuart,* 1976). The difficulty with this test is that there is no uniform rule or standard which can act as a guide. It is merely a judgement call in the particular case which right is to take precedent. Many feel that this is fundamentally no test at all because it is so vague and leaves far too much discretionary power to the judges.

4. *Preferred Freedom Test.* Prior to 1938, legislative action had been given preference over the First Amendment rights of individuals and groups. But in a now famous footnote to a case (*U.S. v. Carolene Products Co.* 1938), Justice Stone stated a position which in effect reversed the burden of proof. The test is based upon the conviction that the Bill of Rights, including freedom of speech, is of such importance that is has a preferred position in relation to other rights. Legislation which invades freedom of speech must involve only the most serious of abuses to permit punishment by the state.

CONCLUSION

The bottom line is quite simple. Either one believes that error can be corrected by debate and discussion or one does not. Such a condition presupposes that men and women will prepare themselves for such discussion, that they want it, desire it, recognize its importance. An introductory class into the art of persuasion is a beginning. When you embark on this odyssey, keep in mind that the theory and practice is ancient. People have fought long and hard for the opportunity to learn, believe, and to communicate to others the results of their convictions. At times it is difficult to maintain the position that in a fair discussion "good" will win over "evil." Not all that we ever imagine or say is sufficiently measured so as to be inherently worthy of public consideration. But it is all we have. Words and symbols can be powerful agents altering emotions and behavior; they can anger and provoke, instruct or inspire. The result is never the same for any one person. However, the invitation to unrest caused by some speech should be desired rather than feared. Either we believe in the capacity of human beings to reason, to contend with what is unsettling, that somehow they will acquire the necessary information to govern themselves, to train themselves for the art of self-government, or this is merely a script where none of us recognize anything and are more given to the freedom of our crimes.

REFERENCES

Baker, R. S. & Dodd, W. E., Eds. (1962). *The new democracy: presidential messages, addresses and other papers.* N.Y.: Hargeer & Crothers.

BeVier, L. R. (1975). The first amendment and political speech: an inquiry into the substance and limits of principle. *Stanford Law Review.*

Brandenburg v. Ohio, 395 U.S. 444 (1969).

Brown, G., Ed. (1977). *Loyalty and security in a democratic state.* N.Y.: *New York Times.*

Chafee, Z. Jr. (1941). *Free speech in the United States.* Cambridge: Harvard University Press.

Civil Liberty Dead. (1918). *Nation, 101.*

Douglass, W. O. (1976). Introduction to a special issue on the first amendment. *Quill, 64,* 8.

Ellis, E. R. (1975). *Echoes of a distant thunder.* N.Y.: Coward, McCann and Geoghagan, Inc.

Emerson, T. I. (1966). *Toward a general theory of the first amendment.* N.Y.: Random House.

Fiske v. Kansas, 274 U.S. 380 (1927).

Isocrates, trans. by Norline, G. (1928). *Antidosis.* Loeb Classical Library.

Meade, G. H. (1934). *Mind, self and society.* Chicago, Illinois: University of Chicago Press.

Meiklejohn, A. (1961). The first amendment is an absolute. *1961 Supreme Court Review.*

Murphy, P.L. (1979). *W.W.I and the origin of civil liberties in the U.S.* N.Y.: Norton.

Near v. Minnesota, 283 U.S. 697 (1931).

Nebraska Press Association v. Stuart, 427 U.S. 593 (1976).

New York Times v. United States, 403 U.S. 713 (1971).

Peterson, A. C. & Fite, G. (1957). *Opponents of war: 1917–1918.* Madison, Wisconsin: University of Wisconsin Press.

Schenck v. United States, 249 U.S. 47 (1919).

United States v. Carolene Products Co., 304 U.S. 144 (1938).

Whitney v. California, 274 U.S. 357 (1927).

Topic Suggestions for Persuasive Speeches

Appendix

A

Classic Controversies
Abortion vs. Right to Life
Advertising—fact or fiction?
Aids testing—Mandatory?
Alcohol and Drug Use and/or Abuse?
American vs. Foreign Education
Birth Control Use in High Schools
Capital Punishment
Cocaine and Crack
Creationism vs. Evolutionism
Discrimination
Divorce—acceptable solution?
Drug Use in Sports
Drinking and Driving
Euthanasia
Free Speech and Responsibilty
Fundamentalism vs. Humanism
Gay Rights
Gun Control
Handicapped vs. Handicapable
Homosexuality—nature vs. nuture
Marijuana Use and Cultivation
Nuclear Weapons or Power
Population Controls
Pornography
Prejudice
Prostitution
Public vs. Private Education
Teenage Parenting
TV Violence—behavioral effects

Medical Issues
Caffiene Consumption
C.P.R. Certification
Dental Care
Dieting for Health

DMSO
Donate Organs
Drink More Water
Give Blood
Herpes Prevention
Preventing Heart Disease
Recombinant DNA
Smoking and Chewing Tobacco
Sodium Intake
Steroid Use
Sugar Blues

Issues from Hobbies
Benefits of
  Athletic Competition
  Dancing
  Dungeons and Dragons
  Exercising
  Fishing
  Golf
  Hunting
  Juggling
  Punk Rock Music
  Rugby
  Sign Language
  Traveling
Magic Tricks in Business—
  How not to get taken
Sports Relieve Stress
Tanning Bed Safety

Environmental Issues
Getting Water to the Desert
Offshore Oil Drilling on the Coast
Old Growth Timber—Save or Log?
Saving the National Parks

University Issues
Collegiate Athletics
Educational Financing
Improving Higher Education
Provide Greater Library Support
Reduce/Increase funding for Athletics

Political Issues
Affirmative Action
Aid to the Contras
Apartheid
Capitalism vs. Communism
Dairy Price Supports
Draft Age—Change?
Drinking Age—Change?
Economic Control and Inflation
Espionage
55 mph Speed Limit—raise?
Foreign Intervention
Human Rights Violation
Military Industrial Complex
Nuclear Arms Race/Talks
Palestinian Liberation Movement
Peace-time Draft
Politics and Evangelism
Political Party Advocacy
Right to Privacy
Strategic Defense Initiative
Trade Tariffs—US policy
Unions vs. Management
Voting Responsibility

Technological Issues
Computers in the Classroom
Computer Industry Explosion
Fuel Exploration
Industrial Pollution Effects
Land Use and Development
Multinational Corporations
Nuclear Power/Weapons
Solar Power—Decline in Research
Wildlife Control and Management
X-Rays are Killing Us

Miscellaneous
Animal Experimentation in Science
Cohabitation vs. Marriage
Commercial Ads are Necessary
Day Care Center Liability
Faculty Tenure
Forestry Issues
Liability of Bars and Taverns
Liberal Arts Education
Money Management
Preventing Insurance Scams
Racial Desegregation
Safety Belt Use—Mandatory?
Semester vs. Quarter System
TV News—Selective Coverage?
Time Management

World Class Excuses for Not Giving Speeches

Appendix

B

"I left my note cards on my father's yacht, which is now headed for the Bahamas."

"I couldn't find anything to wear."

"I ran over my dog which was supposed to be my visual aid."

"My speech is locked inside my car—so are my keys—and the motor is running."

"My hair stylist didn't finish my perm in time. I have a note from her."

"It took me longer to paste-wax my BMW than I thought it would."

"I have a really unfortunate pimple. I'd just die if I had to speak with this monster on my nose."

(In a weak and raspy voice) "I can't give my speech today because I had my tonsils taken out. See? Here they are in this jar!"

"I won't be able to give my speech on Friday because my grandfather is real sick. He's supposed to be better Monday."

"I'm zorry, but I can't teak soday cuz I'm zorta drunk. I jez wanted to not be afraid and now I'm not."

Index

Addams, Jane, 134–135
Alien and Sedition Act, 134
alliteration, 97
analogy, 49
Aristotle, 18, 31, 111
    Rhetoric, 18
attitude, 6
attitude-behavior consistency, 7
audience analysis, 30–37

Baker, R. S., 133
Bartles & Jaymes, 85
Beecher, Henry Ward, 108
behavior, 6–7
BeVier, L. R., 131
Bill of Rights, 137–138, 140
Bombeck, Erma, 32
Borah, William, 135
Brandeis, Louis, 139–140
Brown, G., 135
Burke, Kenneth, 81
Burleson, Albert, 136
Burnett, Carol, 93

card catalog, 42
Carson, Johnny, 73, 105
Carter, Jimmy, 21
Cato, 129
Churchill, Winston, 92, 96
cognitive dissonance, 14
compliance gaining, 4
conclusions, 68–70
connotative meanings, 86–87
Cuomo, Mario, 65, 96

debate, 111–128
Debbs, Eugene, 137
delivery, 99–109
demographics, 30–34
Demosthenes, 81–106
denotative meanings, 86
devil terms, 89

Dire Straits, 31
disinformation, 131
Dodd, W. E., 133
Douglas, William O., 130
Douglass, Frederick, 33, 96
Dubois, W. E. B., 33
dysphemisms, 91

Ellis, E. R., 134
Emerson, Thomas I., 131, 132
Espionage Act, 132–134
ethos, 18
euphemisms, 89–91
examples
    factual, 51
    hypothetical, 52

fallacies of reasoning, 127
Festinger, Leon, 14
Fite, G., 136
Ford, Gerald, 73

Galbraith, John K., 22–23
Geldof, Bob, 27
god terms, 88
Gorbachev, Mickhail, 68
Graham, Billy, 27
Gregory, Thomas, 135, 136

Hart, Gary, 93
Hitler, Adolph, 130
Holmes, Oliver W., 137–138

Iaccoca, Lee, 83
identification, 81–84
introductions, 63–68
Isocrates, 129

Jackson, Henry, 90
Jackson, Jesse, 69, 82, 97
Jefferson, Thomas, 130

Jones, Rev. Jim, 130
Jordan, Barbara, 106

Kennedy, John F., 31, 95, 126
King, Martin Luther, 9, 27, 33, 95, 96, 106

LaFollette, Robert, 135
Letterman, David, 93
Likert Scale, 35
Lincoln, Abraham, 106

Malcolm X, 14, 15, 33, 96
McCormack, Mark, 72
McLuhan, Marshall, 73
Meade, George H., 129
Meiklejohn, A., 132
metaphor, 92–95
mnemonic devices, 60
modifying attitudes, 8–9
modifying behavior, 8–9
Mondale, Walter, 46
Monroe, Alan, 60
Motivated Sequence, 60–62
Murphy, P. L., 134

Nixon, Richard, 17, 126, 140
Norris, George, 135

O'Conner, Sandra Day, 32
organizing speeches, 56–58

parallelism, 96
personification, 97–98
persuasion
    definitions of, 5
Peterson, A. C., 136
Plato, 111
polarization, 91–92
previews, 59
psychographics, 34–37

Qaddafi, Muammar-el, 3, 4
Quintilian, 18

Rather, Dan, 77
Reader's Guide, 42
Reagan, Ronald, 21, 73, 84, 93
reinforcing
    attitudes, 8
    behaviors, 8
repetition, 96
research, 39–44
resolutions, 112–114
reversing
    attitudes, 9–10
    behaviors, 9–10
Richards, I. A., 87–88
Rivers, Joan, 32

Schwarz, John, 47
semantic differential, 35
source credibility, 17–25
speech anxiety, 100–105
Spielberg, Stephen, 72
Stalin, Joseph, 130
statistics, 45–48
Steinham, Gloria, 32
summaries, 59
support, 44–53
surveys, 48–49

testimony, 53
Thomas, Norman, 134
topic selection, 27–30
Toulmin's model, 120–123
transitions, 58
Trudeau, Garry, 52, 64–65
Twain, Mark, 32, 84

Ulery, Bob, 74

Vardaman, James, 135
visual aids, 71–80

Washington, Booker T., 33
Waters, Ida, 134
Weaver, Richard, 88
Webb, Edwin, 135
Webster, Daniel, 39, 99
Wilson, Woodrow, 133, 134, 136

12-15

5   15